THE MERCHANT SAILING SHIP:
A PHOTOGRAPHIC HISTORY

In the late nineteenth century, despite the increasing use of the camera, portrait paintings of sailing vessels became more and more popular. They were usually commissioned by the owners or the master or sometimes by a member of the crew. This typical ship portrait was painted by Eduard Adam of Havre, a well-known ship portraitist, in 1889. It shows the wooden barque *Victoria* built by William Richards of New Bideford, Prince Edward Island, in 1874, and owned by the Richards family until sold to Carl Moller of Drammen, Norway in 1890. At the time this picture was painted the *Victoria* was engaged in trade from Britain to the west coast of South America round Cape Horn. The painting is one of the large collection in the National Maritime Museum.

THE
MERCHANT SAILING SHIP:
A PHOTOGRAPHIC
HISTORY

*127 photographs from the National Maritime Museum
depicting British and North American sailing
vessels and the lives of the people who
worked in and around them*

*Selected and described by
Basil Greenhill, Director of the
National Maritime Museum, and Ann Giffard*

DAVID & CHARLES : NEWTON ABBOT

7153 4685 7

To HAROLD and BERYL SMEDLEY

Set in 11-point Baskerville
and printed in Great Britain
by W J Holman Limited Dawlish
for David & Charles (Publishers) Limited
South Devon House Newton Abbot Devon

CONTENTS

INTRODUCTION

Nearly twenty-five years ago Michael Robinson, then Head of the Department of Pictures at the National Maritime Museum, and I conceived the idea of starting a national collection of maritime photographs in the museum. It was not then widely accepted that photographs would become source material for maritime historians, and interest in the social and industrial history of the nineteenth century was by no means so strong or widespread as it is now. Nevertheless, the immediate response to an initial appeal for photographs, launched through the Society for Nautical Research with the enthusiastic help of Alan Villiers and H. Oliver Hill, was very good. But none of us foresaw that a generation later the photographs would number tens of thousands and their management occupy the full time of two staff members.

The collection is now much used by maritime historians and others but its importance as a record of aspects of British social and industrial history is perhaps not yet widely appreciated. The photographs in this book will convey something of the treasure available. The selection has been made from only one part of the collection, that dealing with merchant sailing ships and the working boats and the life around them. The collection also covers steam and motor merchant vessels and a great part of it deals with the Royal Navy, except for the navy in action in the two world wars. This latter field is covered in great detail in the huge collection of official photographs now appropriately housed at the Imperial War Museum.

Our selection of photographs has been made from the National Maritime Museum collection as it is now and as such it inevitably reflects the deficiencies and the biases of the collection as well as its richness. There is a large number of photographs from the south-west of England. This is partly because a number of collectors, H. Oliver Hill, W. A. Sharman, Michael Bouquet and Dick Gillis among them, have built up libraries of photographs, illustrating the nineteenth and twentieth century maritime history of this area and these people have helped the museum's collection. It is also because in the nineteenth and twentieth centuries the area attracted holiday-makers with cameras and, as the way of life of sail and oar persisted longest in this part of Britain, those who were interested in what was going on around them inevitably recorded it. Some of the resulting records have found their way into the museum—notably the very valuable Fox collection. This Westcountry bias may have been accentuated by our own particular interest in the maritime history of this area.

The museum's photographic archive is still deficient in a number of ways. There are almost no photographs of iron and steel sailing ships under construction in the major ship-building yards and very few interior views of cabins and accommodation, while the photographs illustrating life on board come mostly from collections covering the not altogether typical late nineteenth-century passenger-carrying sailing vessels used partly for training future mates and masters. There are very few photographs of ports, vessels and people of the west coast of North America; there are few photographs of the coal trade. Help in filling these and other deficiencies in the museum's collection will be greatly appreciated.

The photographs chosen for this book include some of the collection's particular gems. The remarkable pictures taken at Swansea in the 1840s show deep, flat-floored, full-bowed wooden vessels of eighteenth-century type which have provoked expressions of disbelief from people familiar only with merchant sailing ships in their latest and most developed forms. The great fleets of large sailing fishing vessels cover the sea more profusely than sailing dinghy classes do at the start of a big race today. Women load slate into a coasting ketch on the open beach at Porth Gaverne. The dock systems of ports, some much reduced in importance today, are filled with the great steel sailing ships of the late nineteenth century, while seaside places, now often without commercial maritime activity of any kind, are packed with smaller vessels. And of course since the merchant shipping industries of the United States and Canada were complementary to that of Britain and many of the advances in the design of sailing vessels and their equipment were made in North America, there are many photographs of North American ships and scenes.

The collection is of technical interest for what it reveals of the details of vessels' rigging and construction and the development of the equipment of ships and boats. It shows how different the sails of merchant vessels and working boats were from the almost standard three-cornered Bermudan sails used in yachts and dinghies today. In only one or two places in the western world were triangular mainsails used commercially in the age of the camera. One of these rarities is illustrated here. Most of the gear on board boats and small vessels could be and was made locally by carpenters and blacksmiths; little or nothing came from a factory. In this way the smaller commercial sailing vessels which still earned their living in the early years of this century could be said to be survivors from before the Industrial Revolution.

But to many people the chief interest of these photographs will rest in the vivid way in which they reveal the changes which have taken place in the last century and a half, indeed in the last seventy-five years, in the conditions of life and work of men and women in the coastal communities, and of men and women at sea. The crews of vessels are shown to have been physically small, sometimes of poor appearance; these photographs showing them at work and play make very clear how different, how immeasurably harder, the lives they lived were from those of any working men and women now. An American shipmaster is seen opening his orders to sail from Bristol, England, to a port which may have been anywhere in the world. He would be out of touch for months on a passage to Callao, San Francisco, Melbourne, or in this case Hong Kong. Cabin passengers, faced with each other's company for months on end, made their own simple entertainment, and ate at a common long table with the ship's master and mates. But the passengers shown in these photographs were a favoured minority—if only photographs could be found showing conditions in the emigrant ships of the 1840s and 50s! Shipwrights were recorded by the camera building and repairing large vessels with hand tools and without the help of any machinery; bargemen can be seen loading their vessels in the space of half one ebb and half the following flood with gravel scooped by shovel from the banks on which their barges lie. By the standards of the late twentieth century the lives of these people were hard, often even cruelly so, but there were compensations which made the life in some ways better than working life ashore. These included a degree of independence and relatively high opportunities for self-advancement among the crews of small merchant sailing ships, though these opportunities did not much offer themselves to fishermen or to the men employed by large shipping companies. There is little of the romance sometimes posthumously associated with the sailing vessel to be seen here.

But how beautiful the ships and boats were! From the spectacular grace of the big square-rigged ships and the great North American schooners to the simple beauty of the lug-rigged boats with everything on board them made by their owners and their gear designed so as not to impede watermen's work and fishing, these vessels had the beauty accidentally generated in some other traditionally designed structures made with limited resources and materials. Only the last big steel and iron sailing ships had much conscious science in their design and construction.

The photographs reproduced in this book have come to the museum through various channels. Some of them are from negatives which have been given to the national collection outright, others have come from generous donors who wished copies of photographs in their own collection to be available to students in the national collection, or they have come from other institutions by gift or purchase. Copies of some of these old photographs exist in more than one collection and although we have tried to attribute them all in the acknowledgments, in some cases their origin is obscure.

Ann Giffard and I are greatly indebted to George Osbon, who is in charge of the photograph collection, for his very material assistance in making this selection of 127 photographs from the thousands available to choose from. H. Oliver Hill, in many ways the father of the collection, has been most generous with advice. We wish also to thank George Naish, Keeper at the National Maritime Museum, Robin Craig of University College, London, and Alan Villiers for considerable help and to thank especially the Trustees of the museum who made it possible for this book to be published.

BASIL GREENHILL

Cotehele, August 1968 - London, May 1969

PROLOGUE

Photography was developed at the beginning of the golden age of the British merchant sailing vessel. While the Royal Navy policed and charted the oceans of the world, the merchant fleet grew steadily in numbers until it was by far the world's largest.

For the first half of the nineteenth century, merchantmen were mostly small wooden sailing vessels. Many vessels, the Blackwall frigates, the Atlantic packets and the early paddle steamers, sailed on scheduled routes. Others, timber-carriers, collier brigs and colonial traders, carried cargoes as opportunity offered, though often principally in one special trade.

In the middle years of the century industrial development in Britain and North America, the expansion of world trade, the growth of Empire, greatly increased the demand for shipping. The repeal in 1849 of the Navigation Laws (which had protected British shipping from foreign competition) and the growth of free trade doctrine spurred British shipowners and shipbuilders to greater competitiveness. By legislation in 1854 designers were freed from limitations imposed by old and restricting ways of measuring tonnage. The economical American-developed schooner rig was widely adopted for small merchant vessels. The Canadian shipbuilding industry, with vast timber resources and low costs, developed and so helped to meet the rapidly increasing British demand for wooden sailing ships. The shipping industry of the United States, devastated by the Civil War, revived and produced the New England built 'Down Easter', the largest of the great wooden square-rigged merchant ships, used principally in the grain trade from California.

As the century wore on new materials, iron and steel in place of wood, wire instead of hemp for rigging, and better canvas for sails, became available. Britain's role of foremost developer of the new shipbuilding techniques again gave her world supremacy; sailing ships became larger and more efficient than ever before. Development culminated in the great steel four-masted barques and ships, 'windjammers' as they were at first derisively, and later nostalgically, called, and in the American and Canadian four- and five-masted wooden schooners.

Steam ships were first built at the beginning of the century, but developed slowly. There were 255 registered at British ports in 1827 but only 624 in 1837. After the development of the efficient compound engine in the 1860s, with the growth of the scale of industry, telegraphs, improved communications ashore and changes in commercial methods, steam ships at last quickly captured world trade so that by 1900 the commercial sailing ship was obsolescent. Nevertheless, she lingered on for half a century more.

During this great period of British expansion, successive Merchant Shipping Acts governed the victualling of vessels, safety regulations, the carriage of deck cargoes and the loading of ships. Samuel Plimsoll is especially remembered for his part in bringing about the passing of the load line legislation. Lloyd's *Register of Shipping*, with its rules for classing ships and their equipment, also helped to improve shipbuilding practice and the lot of the seaman. Thus, just as in the factories and down the mines on land, conditions of life at sea slowly improved.

The photographs in this book illustrate life and ships in this period when the commercial sailing vessels of the western world, after many centuries, developed to their final point in efficiency and size.

TYPES OF SAILING VESSELS AND BOATS

In the course of the nineteenth century it became general, though not universal, practice among those concerned with shipping in Britain, the Empire and the United States to describe sailing ships by their rigs, that is, by the disposition of their masts and sails, rather than by, among other things, their occupations or the shapes of their hulls, as had in general been the earlier practice. During the century these rigs became more or less standardised though numerous exceptions continued to exist and the terms of description were broadly used, thus the term 'schooner' covered very wide variations on a basic theme. The examples illustrated here show the principal types of sailing vessel regularly to be seen in British and North American ports in the age of the camera. In addition, to demonstrate an exception to the rule, the polacca brigantine is illustrated. The terms used to describe the vessels are those which were in general use among shipping people in the latter part of the nineteenth century. There were still considerable variations in the use of this terminology, especially locally.

The terms 'square-rigged' and 'fore-and-aft rigged' are necessarily used. At the cost of some simplification it is fair to say that by the late nineteenth century a square-rigged mast was defined as one divided by its supporting rigging into three distinct parts, a short lower mast, a topmast and a topgallant mast, each with square sails, that is, sails set from yards which could be trimmed on the fore side of the mast only so that the wind propelling the vessel pressed always on the same surface of the sails—the after surface. The fore-and-aft rigged mast was in two parts, a long lower mast and a short topmast, though the latter was not essential to the definition. A gaff and boom sail which could be trimmed only abaft the mast was set from the lower mast and a gaff topsail, or more rarely one or more square sails, was set from the topmast. The gaff and boomsail propelled the vessel by receiving the wind on either side, according to its direction relative to the direction in which the vessel was sailing.

A square-rigged vessel was one with at least one square-rigged mast. A fore-and-aft rigged vessel was one all the masts of which were fore-and-aft rigged. In the later nineteenth century some shipmasters had certificates granted under the Merchant Shipping Acts which qualified them to take charge of fore-and-aft rigged vessels only, some of steamers only, and some of all types of vessel. Only the latter could take command of a square-rigged ship, and this, because the rig was the oldest in descent, the most complex, and the most difficult to manage, was a prestige-conferring qualification in some maritime communities.

Most boats around the coast of Britain were rigged with lugsails or spritsails. These are explained in the descriptions of the photographs in this first section of the book.

1 The Full-rigged Ship

The full-rigged ship, or simply the 'ship' in nineteenth-century terminology, was the queen of sailing vessels, sharing with the brig the longest traceable ancestry. Square-rigged on all her three or occasionally more masts, with a gaff and boom spanker set from the aftermost lower mast, a full-rigged ship of the 1860s or 70s could, and sometimes did, set over thirty-five sails.

The packet ships which sought to maintain scheduled services across the North Atlantic, the Blackwall frigates which traded to India, the majority of the timber and emigrant ships which carried the people who populated North America in the Great Atlantic Migration of the middle years of the nineteenth century, the ships which carried emigrants to Australia

and brought gold and wool home, the tea clippers—nearly all these vessels were full-rigged ships. Thousands more vessels of from 200 to 2,000 tons traded with this rig in every ocean of the world. The wooden full-rigged ship reached her apogee in vessels built in New England and Canada in the middle of the century. By the 1880s huge iron full-rigged ships, nearly 300 ft long, were being built in Britain.

The last full-rigged ship to sail around the world was the British *Joseph Conrad,* a private sail training ship owned and commanded in the 1930s by the seaman-writer Alan Villiers. One of the most beautiful full-rigged ships ever built, she is still preserved afloat at the maritime museum at Mystic, Connecticut.

Joseph Conrad himself was on board the ship illustrated here when this photograph was taken. He was her mate and she was the *Torrens,* a noted ship in the Australian trade, still carrying passengers by the score when this photograph was taken by one of them, Mr Edwards, in the course of a ninety-day passage to Australia in the early 1890s. Part of *Almayer's Folly* was written on board the *Torrens* and it was on a passage home from Australia in her that Conrad and John Galsworthy met and laid the foundations of life-long acquaintance. Conrad himself wrote of the *Torrens* in glowing terms in one of the pieces in his *Last Essays.*

11

2 and 3   The Four-masted Barque   In the late nineteenth century, as the scale of industry and the size of cargoes increased, the standard rig for the big sailing vessel, now grown too large for the three-masted ship rig, became the four-masted barque, square-rigged on three masts, the fore, main and mizzen, fore-and-aft rigged on the last, called the jigger.

The first four-masted barque, the *Columbus*, was built in Canada in 1824. She was a special purpose vessel and it was not until the second half of the century that the rig became established with the *Great Republic* (Plate 2), a huge wooden vessel built at East Boston by the famous Canadian-born shipbuilder Donald McKay in 1853. She carried troops and stores for both the British and the French Governments in the Crimean War, returning to New York in 1856 to enter the Cape Horn trade to San Francisco. The photograph shows her lying in this port in 1860.

After its beginnings in North America, the later use of the four-masted barque rig was a product of the British ship-building industry of the late nineteenth century, made generally possible and profitable by the use of iron or steel for the building of long, narrow hulls of sufficient strength to carry not only several thousand tons of cargo, but also to take the strains and stresses imposed by the rigging transmitting the driving power developed by the huge sails. The steel four-masted barque was an efficient ocean carrier able to compete with contemporary powered vessels in some trades. She represents a considerable technological achievement.

Wooden ships had depended upon flexibility for safety: masts which could be lowered in bad weather, spars which bent, sails which could easily be reefed by big crews. The steel four-masted barque depended upon the strength of iron wire rigging, steel masts and spars, and sails of enormously strong heavy hemp canvas. Major repairs to the rigging required

dockyard plant and the days of the carpenter and blacksmith technology, when a skilled crew could maintain their ship almost indefinitely, were gone for big sailing ships.

Relatively efficient though they were, the last British four-masted barques to be built were launched at the beginning of this century, the last American ones a few years earlier. The last commercial vessel of this type ever to be built was the German *Padua* of 1926. The vessel shown in Plate 3 is the *Routenburn,* built at Greenock by Robert Steele & Co in 1881. At the end of her long life she was owned in Sweden and called *Beatrice.* Some of her fittings can still be seen in the Swedish National Maritime Museum at Stockholm.

4 *The Barque*

The three-masted barque, commonly called simply 'the barque', with fore and mainmast square-rigged and the mizzen with a gaff and boom-sail, developed in the eighteenth century. For the greater part of the nineteenth century this was the most popular rig for what were then medium-sized merchant vessels. By the 1880s the barque rig was found on vessels of any size from 200 to 2,000 tons. The small wooden barque from Britain, from Atlantic Canada, from Norway, was to be met with in every trade which required vessels to carry goods in consignments of a few hundred tons—a scale of business common even in the late nineteenth century. Conrad's *Youth* gives a dramatic description of a passage in such a vessel in her old age.

Wooden barques continued to be built in Finland until the 1920s and a number were engaged in the timber trade from the Baltic to London until the Second World War. Large steel barques carried grain from Australia to British ports until the same period.

The barque in this photograph is the *Asta*, wooden, of 373 tons gross, doubly typical of her type in that she was built in Atlantic Canada (at Maitland, Nova Scotia) and sailed in her later life from Farsund in Norway. She is here shown in the Bristol Channel off Portishead. While in this difficult waterway she has a Cardiff pilot on board and she is towing his cutter down channel in readiness to put him off.

5 *The Barquentine*

Square-rigged on the foremast and fore-and-aft-rigged on her two or more other masts, the barquentine in its modern form was developed on the Pacific coast of North America in the middle of the nineteenth century. The rig was cheaper than the ship or barque, both in initial investment and in maintenance, and barquentines required smaller crews. Although more expensive to build than big schooners of the North American type (see Plate 14)—the foremast of a four-masted barquentine cost as much to install as the total cost of the other three masts—the barquentine was both safer and faster than the big schooner in some trades and the square sails on the foremast were extremely useful on long ocean passages.

Although the rig was always more popular for big vessels in North America than it was in Britain many barquentines were built on both sides of the Atlantic and many square-rigged sailing vessels of other types were converted to barquentines because of the running economies thereby effected. The last British square-rigged sailing ship to operate as a cargo-carrying vessel from a port in the United Kingdom was a wooden three-masted barquentine, the *Waterwitch*, built at Poole in 1871 as a brig and converted to a barquentine in the 1880s.

The barquentine shown here, the *Mozart*, was one of several similar vessels built at Port Glasgow early in the present century.

6 The Brig

The brig, with her two square-rigged masts and the big gaff and boomsail called a spanker set from the main lower mast, was the most popular rig for the larger of the small British sailing ships until the changed economic conditions of the second half of the nineteenth century brought the schooner to popularity. Brigs could be anything from 50 to 150 ft in length and were to be found engaged in every kind of trade all over the world.

Although the schooner was always more common in North American waters, the brig played its part in the development of the United States and Canada. The most famous of all brigs is probably the *Pilgrim* in which Richard Henry Dana spent part of his *Two Years Before the Mast* in the Californian trade from New York.

In British waters great numbers of vessels rigged as brigs carried coal from the Northumberland and Durham coasts to the Thames. An enthralling account of these brigs and the life on board them is to be found in *Collier Brigs and Their Sailors* by the first Lord Runciman who served on board some of them as a boy.

The typical brig illustrated here was Swedish, the *Gerda,* built at Gefle in 1869. Many similar vessels brought timber into British ports from the Baltic.

7 and 8 The Brigantine

The brigantine was a two-masted vessel, square-rigged on the foremast and fore-and-aft rigged on the main. This rig had a long history of development through two or three centuries, while the word brigantine has been used over the same period to describe a number of different kinds of ships and boats. Even in the late nineteenth century the term brigantine meant something different to shipping people in the Mediterranean. In North America at this time the terms hermaphrodite brig or half brig were often used.

Brigantines were usually the smallest type of square-rigged sailing vessel. A well-designed brigantine with her masts and sails nicely proportioned, like the ones shown in these illustrations, was one of the most beautiful varieties of merchant sailing ship. Brigantines were used in general ocean trade all over the world. Large numbers of vessels of this type sailed from British ports on deep water and in the home trade. The rig was much favoured by Canadian builders, particularly in Prince Edward Island in the 1860s and 70s for vessels of moderate tonnage intended for sale in the British market.

Plate 7 shows the world's last commercial square-rigged sailing vessel without an engine, a brigantine called the *Fath ur Bahr* which, owned in the Maldive Islands, was still sailing in the Indian Ocean in the mid-1950s. She was a remarkable survival in more ways than one. She had the deep single topsail with its rows of reef points, a form of sail which had passed

out of general use by the 1870s with the
introduction of the double topsails which
were easier to handle though their gear
was much more complicated, and her
general appearance was that of a vessel of
the 1850s. One of the authors of this book
took this photograph of the *Fath ur Bahr*
as she entered Colombo harbour in
September 1952.

Plate 8 shows the *Elizabeth Maclea*, an
iron brigantine owned in Appledore in
North Devon. She has double topsails.

9 *The Polacca Brigantine*

One of the most interesting of the exceptions to the general statements about vessels' rigs made in this section was the polacca brigantine. Her mainmast had a gaff and boomsail but her foremast was a single pole instead of a normal square-rigged mast and from it only two square sails were set. The rigging of this mast was much simpler than that of the ordinary square-rigged mast. With the aid of big staysails between the masts polacca brigantines were relatively easy to handle in rivers and at sea, even though the hulls of all but the last polaccas to be built were beamy, deep and full-lined.

The polaccas were owned almost exclusively within the limits of the ports of Bideford and Barnstaple in north Devon—chiefly the former—and they were particularly associated with Appledore, a town which is part of the port of Bideford. The origin of the rig has not yet been determined. It has not been positively established that it existed before the 1830s, but the evidence strongly suggests that polacca brigs were sailing from north Devon in the later part of the eighteenth century.

Polaccas sailed in the Mediterranean trade, and from North America, and in the general British coasting trade but they were particularly associated with the carrying of limestone for burning in north Devon kilns across the Bristol Channel from South Wales. A number were built by emigrant Bideford shipwrights in Prince Edward Island, Canada, but most of them were launched from shipyards on the river Torridge at Appledore, at Cleave Houses and at Weare Giffard. The polaccas were the smallest square-rigged commercial sailing ships—for they appear generally though not universally to have been accepted as square-rigged by contemporary authorities concerned with shipping—and a number of them were less than 50 ft long.

The very typical polacca shown here is the *Express,* built at Appledore in 1797. She is loading limestone on the open beach at Lydstep Haven near Tenby in South Wales. The dangerous conditions under which small merchant sailing vessels worked as a matter of course a century ago could not be more vividly illustrated than in this picture.

_10_ *The British Schooner*   While in North America the term 'schooner' unless qualified was taken to mean a vessel with no square canvas at
all (see Plates 14 and 52), in Britain it usually meant a two- or three-masted fore-and-aft-
rigged vessel with square sails set from yards on the fore topmast. Though British schooners
were small they were very numerous. They were of great social importance in that they provided the principal means of income for many seaboard communities and in total they were
of considerable economic significance.

   The schooner can be traced back to a likely origin in the sixteenth century. In the form
shown here schooners came into common use in Britain in the mid-nineteenth century because they were much cheaper to equip and maintain than square-rigged ships and in some
trades more efficient. This schooner is the *Alice Williams*, built at Llanelly in 1854, photographed sailing slowly out of Dover harbour one calm day towards the end of her long hard-
working life. Such heavily repaired sails were unusual.

   In her later life the *Alice Williams* was owned and commanded by Captain Harry Purches
of Par, Cornwall. Shortly after he sold her she was lost on Skokholm Island, Pembrokeshire,
in 1928. The story of her loss and the use put to salvage from her has been told by Ronald
Lockley in his books about his life on the island.

11 *The British Three-masted Schooner* Three-masted schooners were built in the eighteenth century and were in use in the North American coastal trade and the trans-Atlantic trade in the 1830s but the rig did not become common in Britain until the 1870s. From then until the end of merchant sailing ship building in Britain during the First World War, three-masted schooners were very popular with British shipowners, particularly for use in the Newfoundland - Mediterranean trade. Some big two-masted schooners and even some large ketches were re-rigged as three-masters.

The three-masted schooner shown in this photograph of the 1890s is the *Chrysolite* of Penzance, built at Whitehaven in 1869. With her is a small ketch, the name of which cannot be read in the original but which, from her general appearance, has been converted from a smack (see Plate 15).

12 and 13 **The Ketch** The ketch rig in its final commercial form with a tall mainmast and a smaller mizzen, both rigged with gaff and boomsails, developed during the nineteenth century from a number of sources. It had many advantages. Just as the schooner was cheaper to rig, man and maintain than the brig or the brigantine, so a well-designed ketch was cheaper than a schooner. Many seamen maintained that a good ketch was easier to work than a schooner of the same size and safer in bad weather, although they were not so easy to put around when working to windward. Some ketches set square sails on their fore topmasts, a legacy of the smacks from which they were partly descended, and this made them more certain in stays.

In the later nineteenth century ketches became more and more common in Britain both as cargo-carrying vessels and for fishing, and some schooners and many smacks were re-rigged as ketches. Ketches were used in the triangular trade between Britain, Newfoundland and the Mediterranean and numerous different local types of vessel in the home trade were ketch-rigged. Ketches from Appledore in north Devon traded all around the British coasts. The last trading ketch, the *Irene* of Bridgwater, worked (with the aid of a powerful motor) until 1960 (Plate 28).

The very typical ketch shown in this illustration was the *H. F. Bolt,* built by John Johnson at Bideford in 1876 in the yard at East-the-Water which was about to be occupied by H. M. Restarick (see Plates 19 and 20), and named for Captain Bolt's two daughters Harriet and Florence. Plate 13 shows Captain Bolt, his wife and daughters in the 1860s posed in the manner fashionable at the time.

Worn out with years of hard work, the long-lived *H. F. Bolt* fell to pieces when laid up in the River Torridge during the Second World War. She had the distinction of being the last British trading ketch to earn her living without an auxiliary engine.

14 *The North American Four-masted Schooner* As has been seen, in Britain

the schooner developed at her largest and best into a three-masted vessel usually not more than 100 ft long, almost always with square sails on her fore topmast like that shown in Plate 11. In the United States and Canada the three-masted schooner was developed into an efficient and handsome type of vessel three or four times larger with gaff topsails on each mast. Conditions in the long-range coastal trade on the east coast of North America made it possible to develop even bigger schooners. The first four-master built as such was the *William L. White,* launched at Bath, Maine, in 1880 of almost 1,000 tons. Although designed as bulk carriers for special trades, such as the business of carrying coal from Virginia to New England, many of these large sailing vessels were taken up from time to time in the general tonnage market and they were frequent visitors to British ports. Their success stemmed partly from the fact that in the words (written in the late 1940s) of their historian, Captain W. J. Lewis Parker of the US Coastguard, 'no large cargo vessels, whether sail or power driven, have ever been so economical of manpower as these big sailing colliers. In terms of freight capacity they could carry nearly 250 tons more cargo for every crew member than their most efficient rivals in this respect, the present-day diesel cargo vessel.'

As a result of this economy of operation even larger schooners were built. The first five-master was the *Governor Ames* which rounded Cape Horn, and by 1900 six-masted schooners of nearly 3,500 tons were being launched. The largest of all these schooners, the great seven-masted *Thomas W. Lawson,* was almost 400 ft long and one of the three largest sailing vessels ever launched. The only other vessels of comparable size, the *France II* and the *Preussen,* were both square-rigged. Like them, the *Lawson* was awkward to handle in restricted waters, but she was commercially highly successful, paying dividends of 66 per cent of her cost in the first three years of her life. She was lost among the Scilly Isles when on a voyage from Philadelphia to London in 1907 (see Plate 77) and the huge cargo of oil she carried was spewed upon the beaches of Cornwall in a manner which anticipated the *Torrey Canyon* disaster of sixty years later.

In view of the economy with which they could be run it is not surprising that the big North American schooners became the world's last big commercial sailing ships. They continued to be built until after the First World War and the last, the *Adams,* was launched in 1929. Ten years later a large fleet of schooners was still operating on the coast of New

England and Atlantic Canada and across the North Atlantic. The North American schooner did not cease to be a commercial proposition until after the Second World War. The vessel shown here, the *Lilian E. Kerr*, was one of these later schooners. Built in Maryland at Pocomoke City in 1920 and owned in Canada, she was lost in collision while on a passage from New York to Halifax with coal in 1942.

15 The Smack

In the eighteenth century and for the first half of the nineteenth, before the general adoption of the schooner and ketch rigs in Britain, single-masted vessels variously referred to as smacks, cutters and sloops, but most generally by the first term, were the most common small merchant sailing vessels. They existed in numerous forms. Most set a gaff topsail from the topmast and a jib, perhaps also a flying jib from a bowsprit which could be run in on deck when the sloop was entering a small harbour. Some set square sails from the topmast, though this practice became less and less common as the nineteenth century advanced. Smacks 40 or 50 ft long traded to the Mediterranean from south-western England. An Appledore smack, the *Why Not?* brought back a cargo of nuts from Spain as late as the 1890s. Others carried coal and grain on the east coast and yet others were the main means of communication between the mainland and the Scottish islands. Passenger services between London and Scotland, along the south coast and in the Bristol Channel, were run with smacks. They carried the local trade around most parts of the British Isles. Michael Bouquet has vividly described some of these smack trades in his book *No Gallant Ship*.

Trading smacks were still in use at the end of the nineteenth century and a few sailing barges, very similar to the smacks, were still sailing from the Tamar on the Devon-Cornish border after the Second World War. In general, however, the single-masted trading vessel died out with the introduction of the ketch rig in the 1870s and many smacks were re-rigged as ketches.

The smack illustrated here is setting sail as she is towed by local boats out of Porth Gaverne in north Cornwall where she has been loading a cargo on the open beach. The photograph, taken about 1870, illustrates clearly the perilous nature of this smack trade to the beaches of the Westcountry, which remained a normal method of delivering and taking away bulk goods long after the building of the railways. Indeed Appledore ketches were still delivering beach cargoes in the 1930s. That trading smacks often survived for fifty years is an indication of the skill and local knowledge of their masters and the strength of their construction.

16 *The Lugger*

The peculiarly-shaped dipping lug sail, which had to be partly lowered and then reset on the other side of the mast each time the vessel went about, was the most common type of sail used in small and medium-sized fishing vessels in Britain in the nineteenth century. Despite its unhandiness it was a powerful, close-winded and handsome sail, economical because it required only little and simple gear, and it did not clutter up the boat when taken in. It was not suitable for cargo vessels because a big lugsail needed several men to handle it. Fishing vessels carried big crews to handle the nets.

The use of the lug spread and it and its close derivant, the working or standing lug, in some areas replaced the spritsail which had been in use for hundreds of years, and in a few localities it even replaced the efficient gaff sail. The lug did not die out until the general adoption of motor engines for fishing vessels. A well-cut, well-set lug was a beautiful sail. This photograph shows a fleet of fishing luggers from the eastern part of the south coast of Cornwall, each with a dipping lug mainsail and a working lug mizzen.

17 and 18 *The Sprit-rigged Boat and the Lug-rigged Boat*

For most of the nineteenth century the spritsail was the commonest sail in use in working boats, as it had been for centuries before. The sail is a primitive one which seems to have developed at an early stage in a number of widely-separated societies. In its simplest forms it needs no rigging except the sheet. Basically the sprit is simply a means of extending a square piece of cloth to turn it into a sail for running before the wind and the spritsail is used in this way today in East Pakistan, among other places. Sailing to windward came later. The spritsail is extremely cheap and

24

simple and many boatmen could cut it out and rig it up themselves, but it is awkward to reef and to take it in entirely the mast has to be unstepped.

The spritsail in its most developed form survived in the London river sailing barges until the mid-twentieth century, but in smaller vessels and boats it tended gradually to be replaced by the lug during the nineteenth century, especially by the working lug which does not have have to be dipped. This is one of the simplest and most efficient of working sails and because it has neither sprit nor boom it is very flexible in use and very safe. This was important in boats which had to earn their owner's living because a capsize in a heavy boat filled with fishing gear, which represented working capital, and with heavily clothed men who could not swim, was a disaster to be avoided. Indeed, so different from the attitude of the modern dinghy sailor was that of the working boatman that he regarded a capsize as a disgraceful lapse of professional competence, to be concealed as far as possible from his colleagues.

Both these photographs were taken at Appledore at the beginning of this century. The transition from sprit to lug took place late there and there were still a few sprit-rigged boats about until the First World War. Both boats are of the type built and used locally for general watermen's work and for salmon fishing. The use of lug sails as a means of propulsion for working boats at Appledore did not die out until after the Second World War.

THE SHIPBUILDERS

Before the adoption of iron, and in due course of steel, for shipbuilding, wooden sailing ships, large by the standards of their time, were built at yards all around the coasts of Britain. There were centres where the shipbuilding industry was particularly important. London, the Tyne, Sunderland, the twin Shields, Aberdeen, Liverpool, Dundee, Bristol and Bideford were all on their different scales partly dependent on the shipbuilding industry. But full-rigged ships, barques, brigs and schooners for trading all over the world were built at Shoreham and Chepstow, on the beaches of the Isles of Scilly, at Bridport and Topsham, at Portmadoc and Whitby, and in many other places no longer associated with the building of big ships.

Large wooden vessels were built with hand tools and no machinery, without even a permanent shipbuilding site. The ease with which skilled wood shipwrights could build without any facilities is vividly demonstrated by the speed of development of the large ship-building industry which grew up on the beaches of maritime Canada after the end of the Napoleonic Wars. Using timber cut from the adjacent forests, small groups of emigrant shipbuilders, working under totally unfamiliar conditions on the edge of a wilderness, built square-rigged vessels of 200 to 300 tons or more which were laden with timber and then sailed home to England.

In the middle years of the century the great wooden shipbuilding industry in New England developed further and some of the finest wooden vessels ever built were launched from yards in Maine and Massachusetts. Huge wooden schooners continued to be built in these yards until after the First World War.

Iron and steel shipbuilding required much greater capital investment and after 1870 large sailing vessels were built at the centres which developed the new industry, on the Clyde and the north-east coast and on Southampton Water. The building of large steel sailing vessels never achieved the same scale in North America.

But small wooden sailing vessels, brigantines, schooners and ketches for general trade continued to be built in Britain in large numbers and some were still being constructed up to the outbreak of the First World War, many years after the building of large sailing ships had ceased altogether. These small ships were built principally on the west and south coasts of England. It is an indication of the changed nature of the industrial pattern of Britain that Salcombe in Devon, nowadays a holiday resort, had five shipyards at work in the nine-teenth century and as late as 1880 seventy-two sailing vessels were owned there, some of them trading all over the world. At nearby Kingsbridge at least fifty wooden sailing vessels were built between 1830 and 1900.

The photographs which follow show different aspects of the building and repairing of wooden sailing vessels around the coasts of Britain in the age of the camera. They show how vast this vanished and forgotten industry was, how rudimentary was the necessary equipment of the shipbuilder, and how wooden ships were built almost anywhere where there was water, sometimes on an exposed beach below high cliffs or many miles inland on the banks of a tidal river.

19 and 20 *The Vessel in Frame (i)* H. M. Restarick's yard at Bideford East-the-Water in 1879 or 1880, the new barquentine *Winifred* lies off the yard, two vessels are in process of framing up, that is, their ribs have been made and the skeleton is being erected ready to cover with a skin of planks, on the slips behind. They are probably the ketch *Pilot*, launched in 1880, and the ketch *Bessie Clark* completed the following year. A third vessel is hauled out on the marine railway and is under refit. Her name cannot be read but her port of registration is Bideford. Astern of the *Winifred* is a Torridge sailing barge with mainsail set.

The river Torridge, on which Bideford stands, was the home of a considerable local shipbuilding industry for much of the nineteenth century and at times there were seven shipyards operating at once. Square-rigged vessels, large by contemporary standards, were built at Cleave Houses, downstream from Bideford, by George Cox, who moved to the Torridge in the late 1840s from Bridport where he was born in 1810. At Appledore there was a considerable industry in fitting out vessels built in Canada and sailed over for completion on this side of the Atlantic.

George Cox's relative Elias Cox ran a shipyard at Bridport in Dorset (see Plate 21). It was probably through this family connection that H. M. Restarick came to Bideford from Bridport to work for George Cox and eventually to become his manager. When George Cox died in 1877 Restarick took over the yard at Bideford East-the-Water and ran it until 1886. Plate 20 shows H. M. Restarick about the time of the launch of the *Winifred*.

21 *The Vessel in Frame (ii)*

Nestling under the Dorset downs, Elias Cox's yard at Bridport is shown busy with two vessels almost fully framed up. Although the date of the photograph, from the collection of Miss F. M. Reynolds and the Bridport Museum and Art Gallery, is uncertain, it seems likely it was taken in the late 1870s and that the two vessels are, on the right the brigantine *Lilian* and on the left a ketch of the same name, both launched in 1879. The fair taking place by the side of the channel from the harbour to the sea was traditionally held on Whit Tuesday.

In this yard Elias Cox built a large number of ocean-going square-rigged sailing ships. He had close business connections with leading merchants in St John's and Harbour Grace, Newfoundland, whose vessels were employed in the salted-fish trade to Europe. The brigantine *Lilian* was built for Job Brothers of St John's and on her maiden voyage she sailed from Bridport to Cadiz, on to Newfoundland and back to Liverpool all in two months.

Cox's yard was closed down in 1885.

22 *The Vessel in Frame (iii)*

This photograph was taken during the later stages of the framing up of the four-masted schooner *Savannah*, built by David Clark at Kennebunkport, Maine, in 1901. It very clearly shows the mass of timber which went into the building of even a medium size wooden merchant sailing ship. The rider keelson, the second internal keel, is being fitted and an additional balk of timber for this, shaped at the ends to be joined to the other timbers which make up the keelson, is being slung into position.

23 *Planking Up*

Once a vessel's framing was complete she was planked up, that is, covered with her skin. The easiest part of the planking was amidships where the surfaces of the frames were flat. At the stern and bows the steep curves were more difficult to tackle and these parts were often left until last. Here part of the stern planking is still unfinished.

This schooner is the *Two Sisters* and she is being built at the yard of T. Smart & Co of Bosham, Sussex, in the early 1880s. Bosham is now a yachting centre, but at this time it was a distribution point for coal brought round from the North Sea coast in locally-owned schooners and brigantines and Chichester harbour was teeming with commercial sailing vessels.

The *Two Sisters* was still at work in the 1930s; she was broken up after the Second World War.

24 James Goss's Shipyard at Calstock

This shipyard was sited far up the river Tamar, many miles from the open sea. Although always described as 'in Calstock', the yard was on the east bank of the river which here divides Devon on that side from Cornwall on the west bank and it was actually situated in Bere Alston. James Goss was a north Devon man who, having served at sea in square-rigged ships, migrated to the Tamar to work in a relative's shipyard. In due course he set up on his own opposite the then thriving industrial community at Calstock. With his sons he built a number of sailing barges for service on the Tamar and the adjoining coasts of Devon and Cornwall, two ketches, the *C.F.H.* and the *Garlandstone* for general trade, and a large number of boats. James Goss was an extremely industrious and able man; an excellent shipwright, his vessels and boats were well built and handsome in appearance. A number of his boats are still in use on the Tamar, and our own family boat is a replica of one built by Goss about 1908.

His beautiful ketch, the *Garlandstone*, launched in 1909, was among the last wooden merchant sailing vessels to be built in Britain. Like many other shipbuilders James Goss was mainly concerned with maintenance and repair work, and the *Garlandstone* was built as a speculation to provide employment in the winters and when repair work was slack. She took five years to build, five years which more or less coincided with the construction of the Calstock viaduct above the yard. The building of the viaduct was much photographed and in many of the photographs the *Garlandstone* appears as an incidental item. It is possible to follow her gestation in detail. This photograph, taken in the summer of 1905, shows the *Garlandstone* planked up but not yet decked lying on her slipway by the side of a river Tamar teeming with activity.

25 Shipbuilding in Yorkshire in the 1850s This photograph showing a comparatively large vessel in an advanced stage of construction was taken at Scarborough in or about the year 1859. Here, to save rental and space, the vessel is actually being built partly over the water of the harbour. Notice the wooden crane and the piles of planks which are evidently going to be used for planking up the bulwarks and laying the poop and forecastle decks.

26 *A New England Shipyard in the 1870s*

A part of the shipyard of the firm of Goss & Sawyer at Bath, Maine, in 1871. One of the characteristic features of the wood shipbuilding yard was the great jumble of balks of curved timber which lay around in apparent confusion. They were in fact carefully selected for likely future use in making up the frames of vessels and the yard foreman knew the whereabouts of each piece of timber. Around them, as in this photograph, were straight pieces and long sawn planks.

The name of the vessel in frame in this photograph is not known but the newly completed barque is the *Alden Besse,* 842 tons gross. Notice the oxen used for hauling the timber and the mass of wooden chips which paves the building area.

Bath was a great shipbuilding centre and now has its own Maritime Museum to commemorate the industry. Goss & Sawyer were shipowners as well as shipbuilders; a cabin in one of their vessels, the *Guy C. Goss,* is illustrated in Plate 57.

27 *A Vessel about to be Launched*

The barque *Britannia,* here shown almost complete on the slipway at the Old Shipyard at Shoreham, Sussex, was built by Dyer & Son in 1877. She was one of the last two ships to be built at Shoreham which had been a shipbuilding centre throughout the nineteenth century.

The *Britannia* had a life of six years, all of them under the command of Captain Alfred Gasston. During this period she sailed to the West Indies, to India, Burma and Ceylon, to the Falkland Islands and the west coast of South America, to Boston and New York and then to South Africa and Australia, back to Mauritius and then to Liverpool. From Liverpool she sailed to Jamaica, and on her next voyage from Jamaica towards Montreal she was tragically lost on Sable Island.

Such was a fairly typical career for a small wooden barque built in a small port town roughly a century ago. It vividly illustrates an economic, social and technological environment completely remote from the world of today.

28 *The Launch*

A vessel's launch was often a major occasion to be attended by hundreds of people from miles around the shipyard. This was especially so in the smaller shipbuilding communities where a launch was an important economic and social event, all the more so if the vessel, like the *Garlandstone*, had been a long time in the building. The ketch *Irene*, the launch of which is shown here, was built at Bridgwater, Somerset, at the beginning of the present century and her construction was spread over several years. When she was finally completed people came in droves to see her slip into the river Parret on 29 May 1907. Unlike many sailing vessels she was not launched fully-rigged, even perhaps with her sails ready for setting, but a pole was temporarily set up where her mainmast was to be stepped and from it flew a pennant with her name in large letters.

The *Irene* survived to be the last merchant sailing ketch working around the coasts of the British Isles. She ceased to sail in 1960.

29 *The Men who Built the Vessels* The men of Slade's shipbuilding yard at Polruan, Cornwall, photographed in 1867. One shipwright carries an adze, another a plane, a sawyer's boy has a saw. Joseph Slade on the extreme right of the front standing row appears in the original photograph to be carrying a half model of one of the types used in designing vessels. Some of the older of these men were probably born in the eighteenth century. They are respectively:

Back row: Fred Salt, Mathew Salt, Fred Johns, Harry Braddon, Ned Dean, Tom Wyatt, Bert Luxton

Middle row: Charles Wakeham, Albert Pearn, Harry Rogers, Jack Welsh, Sam Slade, Jack Slade, Nat Hunkin, Mark George, Joseph Slade

Front row: Ernest Slade, William Welsh, unknown

The Slades were a shipbuilding family of great repute and one of their schooners, the *Jane Slade,* is recorded by the sailing-ship historian Basil Lubbock as having made the fastest passage ever from the Azores to Bristol.

The wood shipwright developed skill in handling his tools to a point almost unbelievable today, now that we are no longer dependent on such skills. It was said of the best of them that they could cut out the most complex fittings with an adze without taking a measurement or drawing a line. They worked twelve-hour shifts, five days a week, eight hours on Saturday and many of them walked long distances to work before they began. The sawyers were the heart of the yard. All timber for great wooden vessels was cut out by one or two pairs of pit sawyers, the top sawyer standing on the work, the pit boy working in a rain of sawdust underneath. As late as 1900 when a series of large wooden schooners was being built at Appledore there was still no machinery in the yard where they were constructed.

30 The Sail Loft

The sails for new ships and new sails for old ones were made in 'lofts', workshops which tended to be on upper storeys because here there were big open floor areas uninterrupted by stairs and supports for floors above. Sail-making by hand in heavy hemp canvas was a mystery of its own with its own tools and techniques. Sail lofts smelt of tar and new canvas and great bolts of the latter lay around together with coils of rope for the bolt ropes at the edges of the sails. The sailmakers sat on long stools called 'benches'. The ends of these were pierced to take the tools, fids, spikes, grease-filled horns in which needles were kept bright, which the sailmakers used. Other tools and materials were stowed in bags fixed to the bench ends. A good light was essential for sail-making and sail lofts were characterised by their big windows. Old sail lofts, long used for other purposes, can sometimes be detected by these large upper-storey windows.

Treadle machines came into use in the late nineteenth century but inevitably a good deal of hand work always remained. This large loft at Falmouth has only one machine visible and four men at work on benches. Women sometimes worked in sail lofts.

Many skilled seamen could make shift to do entirely satisfactory canvas work; some were quite capable of making any kind of sail. In the ships of the early nineteenth century, and in smaller vessels as long as they were in use, sail-making and repair was one of the many jobs undertaken by master, mate and crew. The big North American schooners rarely carried a sailmaker, depending on the skill of their men and upon shore services for major work, but the large square-rigged ships of the later nineteenth century with their thousands of square feet of sails, each different from the other and in constant need of maintenance and repair, could and did provide employment for full-time sailmakers who were numbered among the vessels' petty officers.

31 A Celebration This photograph came to the museum captioned '"Fairlop Friday", Shipwrights' Outing to Epping Forest'. Five of the men in the model steam launch can be seen to be holding musical instruments and the man in the stern appears to have a conductor's baton in his left hand.

Fairlop Fair, held originally under a great oak recorded as having been 36 ft in diameter with its branches 300 ft in circumference, was founded about 1720 by a Mr Daniel Day, a blockmaker of Wapping, who gave his men an annual bean feast on the first Friday in July. By the middle of the last century the fair was the resort of blockmakers and watermen from all the eastern part of London who paraded in floats like the one shown here and sang traditional songs. Part of the wording of a waterman's song was recorded in 1852 as follows:

> Our horses are all of the very best blood,
> Our boat is well built and her rigging is good.
> With our flags and badges we unanimous agree,
> And join hand in hand to support the old Tree.
> There's old Cruff and young Cruff our music shall play,
> While George Halls' staunch ponies shall tow us away.

32 Ship Repairing in Newcastle in the 1840s

This photograph was taken in Newcastle-upon-Tyne in about 1845. The two men in the foreground appear to be shaping a lower mast from a balk of timber; the gentleman in the tall hat is perhaps the yard owner. The large wooden barque has been stripped down to her masts and is apparently being extensively repaired. This photograph was taken many years before legislation required the painting of a vessel's name on the bows—because of this deficiency it is rarely possible positively to identify the vessels in photographs taken before the 1870s unless the stern happens to be clearly visible.

33 A Vessel in Dry-dock

Wooden sailing vessels were in constant need of repair. Much of this work could be done cheaply by working on their hulls as they lay aground, or upright on the great wooden blocks which were provided for this purpose on many beaches and in tidal rivers. But work under these conditions was slow because it could go forward only at low water, sometimes only for an hour or two each day, and a vessel with big repairs to be done had to sacrifice much earning time.

The two answers to this problem were the patent slip or marine railway, on which the ship was placed in a wheeled cradle which was then hauled out of the water on an incline with capstan or steam engine; and the dry-dock—the latter for large ships only. In this picture the full-rigged ship *Kintore* built in 1870 is undergoing repairs. She is sheathed with metal against the various boring worms which destroy unprotected wooden ships in some waters, and she has the line of painted gun-ports on either side, formal decorations, relics of the early nineteenth century which survived into the twentieth. In the bows are two hold ports, apertures through which long balks of squared timber could conveniently be loaded into the hold while the vessel was afloat.

MADE IN CANADA

A number of references have already been made to sailing vessels built in Atlantic Canada. They played an important part in the British shipping industry in the nineteenth century.

After the Napoleonic wars were over, the Industrial Revolution really began to get into its swing, international trade increased and with it the demand for shipping. But at the same time the trade cycle, that complement of nineteenth and early twentieth century industrial civilisation, began to show itself. Sailing vessels were often slow and port facilities rudimentary. This meant that during a boom period the amount of work a vessel could do was strictly limited by fixed circumstances. Freight rates went up, and owners competed for new ships at high prices. Then the down-swing of the cycle began. Ships took a long time to build and so, as their new ships were delivered, owners soon found themselves with tonnage to spare. Freight rates and ship values dropped and shipowners suffered severe losses. Not only did the shipping industry feel the effects of the trade cycle in a particularly violent form, it was also influenced by events which exaggerated the booms and deepened the depressions. The Californian and Australian gold rushes, the Irish famine, the repeal of the Corn Laws, the repeal of the Navigation Acts, the Crimean War and the American Civil War all had this effect.

The fact that a certain number of vessels were ordered on the upswing of a boom and delivered on the downswing of the following recession was part of the trouble. If reach-me-down, ready-made ships-off-the-shelf could be available in a maritime supermarket where they could be bought, perhaps at high prices, when needed, left in stock when not needed, the violence of the cycles' swings for shipowners could be dampened down. Canadian shipbuilders went some way to fill the role of maritime supermarket between 1818 and 1875. Timber was cheap in Canada, free sites for shipbuilding easy to find, labour was cheap and did not have to be carried in periods of depression. At these times it employed itself on its farms instead of working on vessels.

Canadian ships were good and well-designed, using the latest rigging techniques developed in New England. When they were not selling, the Canadian builder-owners could carry their ships through, largely in the timber trade to Britain, made possible and profitable by the duties placed on Baltic timber to protect the nascent Canadian industry during the Napoleonic Wars and not fully removed until 1860. The timber trade was a one-way traffic, vessels sailed west with empty holds and their owners were very ready to offer cheap passages. The majority of the emigrants who travelled from Britain to North America in the Great Migration of the mid-century did so in the holds of timber ships.

So Canadian sailing-ship building, the prosperity of the British shipping industry, the timber trade from Canada to Britain and the peopling of the North American continent are linked together in the maritime history of the nineteenth century.

34 Loading Timber at Quebec A large, typically Canadian-built, wooden full-rigged ship loading small timber through bow ports in the St Lawrence at Quebec. Tackles have been rigged on the forecastle head for lifting the timber to the ports and swinging it into the hold. The jibboom, the spar which projects beyond the bowsprit, and the martingale, the light spar projecting downwards which helps to hold the jibboom down, have been run in so that the vessel will take up less space at the crowded moorings.

The ship is the *Parramatta,* built in 1853 at Kingston, New Brunswick.

35 *The Barque Mizpah*

In relation to its size and population the tiny colony of Prince Edward Island, now Canada's smallest province, was the most productive shipbuilding area in Canada. In *Westcountrymen in Prince Edward's Isle* we have told some of the story of how this came about. Though the average size of Prince Edward Island vessels built for export was smaller than that of the products of Nova Scotia and New Brunswick, many large full-rigged ships, barques and barquentines were launched in the Island, which continued building wooden sailing ships until 1920.

This photograph shows a typical Island barque, the *Mizpah*, built in 1876 at Grand river in Prince county at the western end of the Island by John Plestid for John Yeo and later sold to Norwegian owners. John Yeo, who later became a senator of Canada, was the youngest son of James Yeo, greatest of the Prince Edward Island shipbuilders.

36 The Barquentine Raymond

Typical of the smaller vessels built in Prince Edward Island for sale in the British market was the barquentine *Raymond,* built as a brigantine at Summerside, Prince county, by John Lefurgey. Here shown making sail as she leaves Fowey deep-laden astern of a tug, she was still afloat during the Second World War, the last surviving representative of Canada's contribution to Britain's nineteenth-century shipping expansion. (Illustration on facing page, below.)

37 The Full-rigged Ship Regent

In the 1870s and 80s, the last years of the building of large wooden square-rigged sailing ships, some particularly fine vessels were launched in Nova Scotia and New Brunswick which had supplied the British market with many large square-rigged vessels in earlier years. This photograph shows the full-rigged ship *Regent,* built at Avondale, Nova Scotia, in 1878 by J. A. Harvie and sold to Andrew Gibson of Liverpool, England. The *Regent* traded all over the world and even in her old age was able to hold her own with much more modern sailing vessels. Notice the wooden platforms outside the hull to which the standing rigging which supports her masts is set up. These were called 'channels' and were characteristic of large wooden vessels, helping to distribute the stresses more evenly over the fabric of the hull.

The *Regent* is shown discharging a timber cargo from Pictou, Nova Scotia, at Bristol in August 1907. Shortly afterwards she was broken up.

THE MASTER

At the beginning of the age of photography the master of a merchant sailing ship was still very much the controller of his own and his owner's fate. Before the trans-oceanic telegraph lines were laid a vessel's arrival back in Britain frequently brought the first news of her outward passage. The master was both the bearer and the interpreter of his instructions and as no one could foresee all the circumstances he was likely to meet, his instructions were frequently in very general terms. The owner was in the master's hands. As Professor Ralph Davis has put it:

> ...The greatest problem of management, indeed, can be put in a nutshell; to find a paragon to be master, and then devise means to assist him if he really were perfect, rescue him if he turned out a fool, and then restrain h:m if he turned out a scoundrel...

In early years they were men without paper qualifications. Not until the middle of the nineteenth century was a system of compulsory examinations for masters and mates instituted in the Merchant Shipping Act of 1850. For years afterwards many masters sailed on certificates of service granted under the Act to men already experienced in command at sea who had not passed the new examinations. Some of them could scarcely read or write and their navigation methods were simple. Yet some of them conducted their vessels about the world to their owners' and their own considerable profit. For the system could be very rewarding to an enterprising master who, first buying shares in a vessel, could prosper to the point of becoming a principal owner himself and in due course settle as a capitalist ashore. Many masters did this—some built up considerable fortunes.

In later years, with improved communications and greater regulation, the master's position became less independent, less responsible and less rewarding, and in the big sailing ships of the later nineteenth century it was only the very exceptional man who was able to break away from being an employee. In the later days of the sailing ship the masters of big vessels were often not well-rewarded for the enormous responsibility they carried and the great professional skill they had to display to bring about the successful completion of each passage.

38 The Master of a Clipper

William Stuart, master of *The Tweed,* a famous full-rigged ship of the 1860s, was photographed in Melbourne in 1887. Joseph Conrad records in *The Mirror of the Sea* that she once beat the steam mail-boat from Hong Kong to Singapore by a day and a half. William Stuart was probably the original of Conrad's 'Captain S—' who commanded *The Tweed* on some of her finest passages and was so disappointed with his failure to obtain an equal performance from his next ship.

David MacGregor, a historian of British merchant sailing-ship design, has recorded that the tea clippers *Cutty Sark*, *Blackadder* and *Hallowe'en* were all built as copies in greater or lesser degree of *The Tweed*.

39 and 40 Masters of Timber Ships   This remarkable photograph, taken in Quebec, apparently in the early 1840s, shows two shipmasters who have been identified by descendants of one of them as William Yeo and Richard Williams. Other evidence supports this identification. William Yeo was master of the *Five Sisters*, a barque built and owned by his father James Yeo of Port Hill, Prince Edward Island. Richard Williams was mate of the vessel under Yeo and later became master of the Yeo's brig *British Lady* and their barque *Mary Jane*, all Canadian-built and employed in the timber trade to Britain.

Yeo and Williams were both born in the same year, 1811, Yeo at Kilkhampton in Cornwall and Williams at Appledore, across the Devon border. William Yeo returned to Appledore and there established himself as his father's British agent. He died in 1872 a very rich man and one of the principal shipowners of south-western England. Williams died at Quebec in 1851 at the age of 39.

This must be one of the oldest-surviving photographic portraits of merchant shipmasters. It is made the more interesting by the survival of a portrait of Captain Williams' wife, Harriet (Plate 40), grandmother of Harriet and Florence Bolt for whom the *H. F. Bolt* (Plate 12) was named. Such was the interlocking pattern of family and business relationships in a nineteenth-century seafaring community.

41 The Master of a Small Deep-Sea Sailing Vessel

Jabez Hocken of Newquay, Cornwall was master of the schooner *Julia* of Padstow, built at Padstow in 1879. In her he sailed regularly in trade between the Mediterranean and North and South America. He held a master's certificate for fore-and-aft rigged vessels only, which is now preserved in the archives of the National Maritime Museum and he enjoyed something of a reputation as an exacting and meticulous shipmaster.

The accounts of some of his voyages in the *Julia* are in the possession of Mr Richard Gillis of Newquay, Cornwall. They show the *Julia* to have been a very profitable vessel. Captain Hocken was paid 14s per day to take the *Julia* backwards and forwards across the North Atlantic and for the 384 days from 23 April 1891 to 10 May 1892 he received £276 16s in salary. In addition to this sum, however, he had various perquisites and he was a shareholder in the vessel. His total income made him one of the more prosperous members of his local community.

42 A Master in the Home Trade

William Kingdon Slade of Appledore, born in the 1860s, was the son of a deep-water seaman in square-rigged ships in the North Atlantic trade. He went to sea himself in square-rigged ships and after acquiring wide experience took a job in the home trade as master of an Appledore ketch, the *Francis Beddoe*. Although he had no certificate and was only partly literate, he soon became a shareholder and in due course principal owner of sailing vessels in the home trade. He was a driving, energetic man and an extremely competent shipmaster. His family established themselves as the last owners of a fleet of commercial sailing vessels in Britain.

THE MEN

The composition of the crews of merchant sailing ships in the nineteenth century varied greatly with the years and with the type, home port, and ownership of the vessels and the kind of work in which they were employed. Very generally speaking, in the early years of the camera vessels tended to have among their crews a high percentage of men from the neighbourhood of the small ports from which many of them still sailed. But as the scale of the shipping industry grew in the latter part of the century the crews of the larger ships were recruited much more widely. As the standard of living and opportunities of employment ashore improved fewer men went to sea from Britain and many of those who did so were drawn by the greater safety and comfort of steam vessels.

Some later professional sailing-ship seamen were rootless wanderers of the type so brilliantly depicted by Joseph Conrad in *The Nigger of the Narcissus*—there were many foreign seamen among the crews of the later British sailing ships. Recruitment to the ranks of the mates and masters of big vessels largely ceased to be made from among the seamen. Where a good system of apprenticeship existed, as it did in a few shipping companies, boys and young men who had already completed their secondary education were given experience as seamen and some opportunity to study for their professional qualifications.

Life at sea, like life for people in comparable employments ashore, was poor and hard in the early years of the century. Rising economic prosperity, government legislation, the requirements of the insurance-classification organisations, a developing social conscience, all worked together to improve conditions at sea as the century advanced, as they did similarly to improve industrial conditions ashore. But although a seaman in a schooner sailing from the port in which he was born was often as well housed as, and better fed than, an agricultural worker ashore and had a far better chance of breaking out of the perpetual treadmill of the labouring life, the men in big square-rigged sailing ships followed an arduous calling with little or no prospect of improvement. These men accepted industrial conditions which would be inconceivable today.

43 Scots Fishermen of the 1840s

No photograph in the great collection in the museum conveys more strikingly the social changes that have taken place since the middle of the last century than this one taken by the great Octavius Hill. It shows Newhaven fishermen in canvas trousers and short jackets, one wearing a wide-brimmed tall hat. These clothes are indistinguishable from those of merchant seamen and naval ratings of the period.

44 *The Crew of a Barque*

This is the oldest of the photographs of crews in this book. The name of the vessel is not known but she is believed to have been a steel or iron barque sailing from Aberdeen, and the photograph was taken about 1890. The men are of small stature, though powerfully built. Apart from a tendency to effect peaked caps, there is little to distinguish them from labourers of the same date ashore.

These men probably lived in a forecastle compartment below the main deck right in the bows of the vessel and sometimes shared with the windlass. Such 'forecastles' can still be seen today in the full-rigged ships *Cutty Sark* at Greenwich and *Charles W. Morgan* at Mystic, Connecticut. The crew of Conrad's *Narcissus* can be imagined to have looked very much like these men. Later, living conditions improved and seamen were accommodated in houses on the foredeck. Some of the later four-masted barques had crew accommodation in a midships house which was dry, safe and relatively comfortable. In some of the later big North American schooners the crew's accommodation was even equipped with central heating, driven from the boiler which supplied the steam machinery for setting the huge sails.

45 *Officers of the Port Jackson*

The four-masted barque *Port Jackson* was built at Aberdeen by Alexander Hall & Company in 1882 and has been described as one of the most beautiful iron vessels ever built. She was principally employed for most of her life in the Australian trade to Europe, first as an ordinary working cargo vessel and later as a cargo-carrying training ship for future mates and masters. She was torpedoed in 1917.

This photograph shows one of her masters, Captain Maitland, with some of his mates and other officers at lunch in the saloon.

46 *Seamen at Work*

These men of the iron full-rigged ship *Loch Tay*, built in Glasgow in 1869 for the trade to Australia, are splicing wire rope—maintenance work on the standing rigging. Notice the great fly-wheel with curved spokes on one of the hand-driven pumps at the foot of the mainmast and the cages in which the livestock was carried for food on long passages, securely lashed with ropes on top of the main hatch.

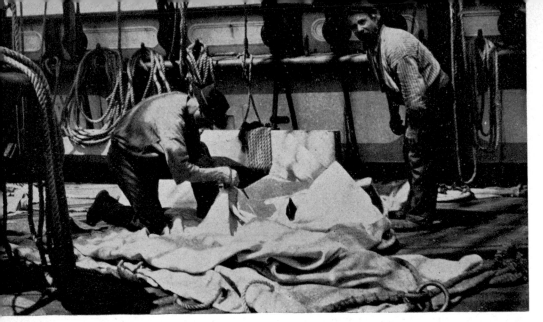

47 The Sailmaker Another photograph taken on board the *Loch Tay* shows the sailmaker at his work of repairs. Exceptionally, he is not sitting on his bench but he has the leather palm on his hand to protect him when he pushes the great needle through the heavy canvas. The sails on this big iron ship are sewn into iron-wire bolt ropes with steel or iron rings at the clews, the lower corners.

48 An Extempore Band On long voyages the crews of merchant sailing vessels entertained themselves in various ways. In many ships bands were organised. Here on board a Loch Line sailing vessel there are visible a mouth organ, an accordion, a washboard, castanets, two flutes and a jew's-harp. The clothes seem to be a mixture of working gear and fancy dress put on for the occasion.

49 *The Crew of a Schooner*   The wooden three-masted schooner *Earl Cairns* was built at Connah's Quay in 1883. This photograph was taken probably in the 1920s when she was still busily employed in the home trade. These men, who have not been identified but some of whom are almost certainly still alive, were the last exponents of the skills needed to maintain and sail a small wooden merchant sailing ship, heirs to techniques and attitudes of mind older than those of the crew of the *Loch Tay* many years before and going back to an earlier kind of seafaring.

They slept on canvas-frame folding bunks in a 'forecastle' below the deck right in the bows beneath the windlass. It was heated by a coal stove. All the crew including the master ate together in the panelled cabin in the stern of the vessel and here the master and perhaps the mate as well had tiny cabins fitted with locker bunks let into the side of the schooner. Their food was generally better than that provided for the seamen in large square-rigged sailing ships. A favourite dish in the home trade was 'schooner-on-the-rocks'—beef served on top of boiled potatoes—but on the long voyages westwards across the North Atlantic or to South America most meals, of course, comprised basically salt-preserved meat and fish.

WOMEN AND THE SAILING SHIP

Since the sailing vessel was the principal means of sea transport for much of the nineteenth century, women were inevitably concerned with it in various ways, directly and indirectly. As the next section of this book will show, they travelled as passengers in large sailing ships engaged in regular passenger service. Thousands upon thousands of them travelled as emigrants to North America, Australia and New Zealand. For outlying coastal communities sailing vessels were frequently the only means of communication with centres of population, and in the early part of the century even to travel from Edinburgh to London, from Bideford to Bristol or from Plymouth to London was quicker and more comfortable in one of the regular sailing vessels than by coach. Island communities depended on the sailing vessel for connection with the mainland. Sailing boats were employed at every long ferry across an estuary; even women from inland inevitably came into contact with sailing vessels whenever they travelled for long distances.

But women were much more intimately concerned with sailing vessels than this. Sometimes the wives of illiterate owners of small merchant schooners and ketches did all their husbands' business for them. The rise into prosperity of many families concerned with the ownership of small sailing vessels can be traced to an energetic, managing wife. The age of photography overlapped by many years the period when women were still doing heavy labouring work, skilled and unskilled. Annie Slade, wife of William Kingdon Slade, whose photograph appears in the section on The Master, was the daughter of the master and part-owner of a trading smack. When for one reason or another there was a shortage of manpower in the family to sail the smack, Annie, as was the local custom, went along with her father as the third hand. More than once in later years she acted as crew for her husband. Women worked at loading and discharging vessels in port and there were even women sawyers in the shipyards of the mid-1850s.

50 *Women and Pleasure Sailing* At fashionable yachting centres women came into a somewhat unreal contact with sailing vessels; at more informal places they could become more involved with pleasure sailing. We chose this photograph, taken in Ilfracombe harbour at the end of the last century, partly because the mixed party look as though they were out to enjoy themselves and partly to show the beauty and complexity of a nineteenth-century small yacht with her gaffsail, jackyard topsail, bowsprit and two headsails and her straight stem and shapely counter. The name of the professional hand standing in the stern is given as Nichol Barbeary.

51 *Women Use the Ferry* To travel from Appledore to Instow in north Devon in 1900 meant either a long journey round by Bideford bridge, taking more than an hour by horse transport, or a short sail across the Torridge in 'Daddy' Johns' sprit-rigged ferry boat. At the beginning of this century these ladies chose the second alternative, although nothing they wore was in any way suitable for travelling by sailing boat. They wait on the ferry slip while Mr Johns prepares their vehicle.

52 The Sailing Vessel as Omnibus Countrywomen living in isolated coastal communities or on islands used the service provided by small sailing vessels to reach the nearest centre of population. This was nowhere more true than in Newfoundland where small schooners were still a principal means of communication until the middle of this century. The *Elizabeth*, a typical small North American schooner with no foretopmast and simple rigging, has on board a number of passengers including at least five women. Notice how the oat in which two men and a boy are coming ashore is being sculled through a hole in the transom.

53 *Women Loading a Vessel*   This remarkable photograph taken in the early 1870s shows a gang of women stevedores loading slate from the Delabole quarries in north Cornwall into a ketch on the beach at Porth Gaverne. The men lift the slates from the carts to the vessel's side and the women then raise them to the hatchway. The actual stowing of the slates in the hold was probably done by the vessel's crew. At Appledore, where the census of 1851 shows large numbers of women employed as 'limestone porters', that is, as stevedores to discharge the limestone brought over from South Wales in polacca brigantines, the women worked down in the hold lifting the stones while the men on deck slung them over the side. The women would roll the heavy stones up over their knees and then lift them in their arms up to a man on a plank in the hatchway who threw them on the deck for another man to roll over the side.

PASSENGERS UNDER SAIL

Despite the greater comfort and convenience of steamships, which took over the North Atlantic emigrant trade as early as the 1860s, sailing vessels continued regularly to carry cabin passengers until late in the last century and, because the long haul made them competitive with steamships, a superior class of emigrant sailing vessel survived in the Australian trade until the 1890s.

There were several reasons why cabin passengers should travel under sail. A sailing vessel passage was cheaper than one in a steamship; in many ways it was an extremely pleasant and always an interesting experience for those inclined to make their own entertainment and with time to spare. A passage in a great sailing ship had on a gigantic scale some of the elements which attract people today to small-boat cruising. Doctors used to recommend sailing-vessel voyages to patients in need of rest or (a fashionable recommendation for tubercular patients at the time) of life in the open air.

54 A Group of Passengers
This photograph was taken by the master of the *Macquarie*, Captain Mumford, showing a group of first-class passengers and some of the mates gathered by the break of the poop. The *Macquarie* was a famous vessel in the Australian trade and these people must have spent some three to four months in each other's company on the voyage, living in conditions which in good weather were very comfortable by the standards of their times.

55 *On the Poop Deck* Much of the passengers' time would be spent in reading, eating and sleeping, in keeping diaries (some passengers' diaries are fascinating social history), and in long, long conversations. This photograph, also taken in the *Macquarie,* shows passengers on the poop in good warm weather, calm seas and light breezes. Awnings have been rigged against the sun. The vessel appears to be on the port tack. Most of these passengers will have to move if an occasion arises for trimming the sails.

56 Deck Games   Entertainments were simple and do-it-yourself. This photograph was probably taken on board the iron full-rigged ship *Superb,* built at Blackwall in 1866 and owned in Liverpool. It is good weather and deck games have been organised which both passengers and crew join in together.

57 Accommodation Below Decks   This photograph shows the accommodation under the poop of the *Guy C. Goss,* built at Bath, Maine in 1879 and said to have been the largest wooden barque-rigged vessel under the flag of the United States. The accommodation is relatively luxurious, roomy, panelled, with pilasters and engraved glass, organ and plush sofa, all the contemporary trappings of a prosperous society.

THE SAILING VESSEL AT SEA

Each passage in a sailing vessel was an adventure of indefinite duration. On the shorter passages, as across the North Atlantic, only the most general predictions of likely weather could be made. On the long hauls, the Australian trade, the trades to the west coast of America, to India and the Far East, reasonable assessments of the conditions likely to be met with at different stages could be made by skilled masters. But such was her vulnerability to the sea and the weather, and so complex and relatively frail was the sailing vessel's gear, that almost any problem could and often did present itself to her master on any passage anywhere.

58 *The Master of the American full-rigged ship A. G. Ropes receives his sailing orders*
The *A. G. Ropes*, a magnificent wooden full-rigged ship built in 1884, was for a time the finest vessel of her class under the US flag. She was commanded throughout her life by Captain Dave Rivers, and in this photograph he is seen opening his orders to sail from a British port while interested shore folk look on. The orders were to load coal for Hong Kong.

The *A. G. Ropes* was one of the great wooden square-rigged vessels built in New England to meet the demand for ships to export grain from San Francisco to Europe, a trade which was very prosperous in the late 1870s and the 1880s. These vessels, known from their ports of origin as 'Down Easters', were very strongly built, fast yet economical, and able to carry large cargoes. Except for the later Canadian and United States barquentines, they were the last class of wooden square-rigged merchant sailin ships to develop. After them, and overlapping to a considerable extent, came the great North American schooners which are illustrated in this book.

59 *The Illawarra goes to Sea*

For raising the anchor in the later big sailing ships a capstan on the forecastle head was geared to the windlass situated in the forecastle below. Some of these big ships had steam available to drive a small engine to work the windlass, but in others the traditional massed manpower of the whole crew was used, slowly and laboriously, to haul the vessel up to her anchor and then break it out and bring it to the waterline, from where it was lifted up to the forecastle head by means of a tackle or an anchor crane. Such methods of work, when the alternative of investment in steam donkey engines was open to owners, indicated that manpower and time were both cheap.

This work at the capstan bars was one of the aspects of a sailor's life which caught contemporary attention, partly because it involved simple movements readily intelligible to the landsman and partly because it was sometimes accompanied by working songs. These were the shanties which helped to co-ordinate the efforts of the men.

This photograph was taken on board the iron full-rigged ship *Illawarra*, built in 1881 at Glasgow and engaged in the Australian trade with passengers and cargo. Notice the ship's bell with her name, date of building, and port of registration.

60 *Illawarra* The work in the rigging aloft was of course a very important part of the life of the crew of a sailing vessel. Its extent and difficulty depended on the rig and type of vessel. In a wooden square-rigged ship of the first half of the nineteenth century, with rigging made largely or entirely from natural fibre, the sheer work of maintenance, quite apart from the handling of the sails, upper masts and yards, was endless and called for highly developed technical skills. The iron and steel vessels of a later period with metal masts and spars and rigging made mostly of wire and chain required less maintenance and could be handled by smaller crews despite their greater size. In the big North American schooners there was relatively little work to be done off the deck, but what there was was difficult and called for a very high degree of skill because of the absence of hand and foot holds in the simple rigging and the difficulty of handling the great gaff topsails, so much less controllable than square sails set from yards.

This photograph shows a seaman's-eye view looking down on the fore side of the mainmast from the fore topgallant mast in the full-rigged ship *Illawarra*. The ropes for furling the mainsail can clearly be seen running across the fore side of the bulging, wind-filled canvas.

61 *Macquarie (i)* The ship is braced up on the starboard tack in a smooth sea with a
breeze blowing. The sun is shining, a passenger is strolling on the
main deck and a hand is cleaning out one of the boats. These are ideal sailing conditions
and Captain Mumford found time to take this photograph from the emergency lifeboat which
the *Macquarie* carried slung outboard on the starboard side of the poop. Notice the painted
gunports on the vessel's side.

62 *Macquarie (ii)*   On long voyages sails were changed to suit weather conditions, heavy new sails were used in zones of predictable strong winds, old and worn or lighter and cheaper sails in areas of prolonged light winds and summer conditions. The weight of the sails on big vessels was in proportion to their enormous size and there were often thirty or more of them to be changed, usually twice on a voyage to Australia, each secured to the yards or stays with numerous robands or hanks.

This photograph by Captain Mumford shows the crew at work changing the mainsail of the *Macquarie*. Above them around the mast is the semi-circular platform of the maintop, used to spread the shrouds to support the topmast and as a working space. To avoid the necessity of climbing round the overhang made by this top when going aloft to the higher rigging square holes have been made. This was by no means always done (see Plate 70).

63 Lee Fore Brace

Part of a watch is hauling on the lee fore brace on board an unidentified steel or iron square-rigged vessel. There is a lot of wind and some sea and the vessel is on the starboard tack. The lee fore brace, led as it was to the lowest part of the main deck, provided a wet and nasty and sometimes dangerous job if the fore yards had to be trimmed when seas were breaking on board.

64 Main Deck of the American ship A. G. Ropes in a fresh breeze

The great *A. G. Ropes* (see Plate 58) is sailing fast with a strong breeze on her starboard quarter. The typically American deck-house fo'c'sle in which the crew lived can clearly be seen. This sort of accommodation was considerably more comfortable than the fo'c'sle right in the very bows where the crews of many British vessels of comparable size were accommodated.

65 *Port Jackson*

Taken from the bowsprit netting, this magnificent photograph shows the whole length of the decks of the iron four-masted barque *Port Jackson* under the shadows of her swelling sails.

66 *Camborne*

By way of contrast, this photograph was taken from the bowsprit of the British wooden three-masted schooner *Camborne* built at Amlwch in 1884. The vessel has her flying squaresail set from the fore yard and a strong wind on her starboard quarter. The *Camborne* spent most of her life in the home trade about the British Isles and nearer continental ports and was owned for many years by Captain Hugh Shaw of Arlingham in Gloucestershire. Captain Shaw has deposited a typescript account of his life in her and in other sailing vessels in the National Maritime Museum, one of the very few first-hand accounts of this kind of seafaring life under sail.

67 On board an American Four-masted Schooner at Sea

The four-masted schooner *Marjory Brown* was built at Wilmington, Delaware in 1889 by Jackson & Sharp. This photograph, taken from her mizzen rigging on a calm, misty day at sea, shows the tall lower masts, the hoops which held the long straight luffs of the great gaff sails to the masts, the jaws of the booms and the arrangement of the decks with the long poop with deck-houses half sunk into it. Two of the crew, one in a bowler hat, are conversing on deck.

The general appearance of the *Marjory Brown* was similar to that of the *Lilian E. Kerr* illustrated in Plate 14.

68 Entering Harbour

Paddle tugs came increasingly into use from the 1820s onwards, and Plate 79 shows some splendid examples dating from the 1830s. Although for reasons of economy the masters of sailing vessels avoided using them whenever possible, the tug was really essential to the operation of the four-masted barque or the big North American schooner in restricted waters, while to enter some harbours a tug was necessary for most vessels except under ideal conditions.

The big clinker-built wooden tug *United Service* is here shown towing an unidentified brigantine into Gorleston on 9 March 1897.

The *United Service* herself was built at North Shields in 1872 and owned in Yarmouth all her seventy years of life. Primarily a tow boat she was used for pleasure trips in summer. In October 1891 she towed the Caister lifeboat *Godsend* through heavy seas to the assistance of the ketch *Brightlingsea* which had gone ashore near the Wolf lightship.

A SAIL TRAINING SHIP AT SEA

In the mid-twentieth century a few sailing vessels still work for their livings. On the coast of New England, in the West Indies and the Mediterranean, sailing cruises have become popular and profitable and in New England in recent years a number of reproductions of small American merchant schooners have been built for this trade. Schooners and square-rigged vessels built to resemble late nineteenth-century merchant ships are used by some educational establishments preparing young men for a seafaring profession in a number of countries of the world.

Some years ago one of us was fortunate enough to be able to make a number of short passages in one of these latter vessels, the Japanese four-masted barque *Nippon Maru*. The photographs which follow show something of the life and work on board a modern sailing vessel built like a merchant sailing ship. They can be contrasted with the photographs taken on board merchant vessels which appeared in the previous section.

69 The Kaiwo Maru

The four-masted barques *Nippon Maru* and *Kaiwo Maru* are almost identical. They were built at Kobe in 1930. 250 ft long, they are of over 2,000 tons gross. The mainmast is 164 ft from truck to keel and the main yards are 76 ft long. Each has twin diesel engines of 600 horse power each, giving a speed under power of about 10 knots. They carry over sixty cadet deck officers and fifteen engineer officers and ratings, seven deck officers, six cooks, three pursers, three radio operators and a doctor, twenty-one professional sailing-ship seamen and four boys. Both ships usually make a trans-Pacific voyage to the United States or Canada via Hawaii in summer after shorter working-up voyages in the spring. In the winter they operate under power. They work in a pattern of professional education which includes a number of training ships without sails, two sea universities giving courses up to degree standard, and five sea secondary schools. The whole system is government financed and controlled.

The *Kaiwo Maru* was photographed in Tokyo Bay.

70 Cadets going Aloft

Cadets going over the maintop. There are no holes in the platform and the men going aloft must cope with the overhang, which has deliberately been made less steep than it was in most merchant vessels.

71 From the Jigger

This photograph was taken from the crosstrees on the jigger mast when the vessel was sailing with a nice breeze on the beam. The great size of the masts and yards and the complexity of the gear are very apparent.

72 *A Pull on a Brace*

There is no deck machinery in *Nippon Maru;* all the hard work is done by groups of cadets. Here part of a watch is pulling on a brace to swing round one of the lower yards while the vessel is going about. All work of this kind is carried out with great zest and enthusiasm.

73 *Making fast a Sail*

Cadets soon become confident at work aloft, though the man balanced on top of the yard is probably one of the professional seamen. They are making fast the foresail, passing the gasketts around the folded canvas and the yard. They stand on the foot ropes, lean against the yard, and are free to keep hold of the jackstay with one hand. The *Nippon Maru,* like a later merchant ship, does not have the safety devices—arm loops secured to the jackstays, back ropes—used in some European training ships, but accidents are extremely rare.

THE PILOT CUTTER

When she approached land the master of the big deep-sea sailing vessel needed the services of a local pilot to take him through relatively-restricted waters into harbour. To get him to the big ship the pilot had his own transport which could vary from a 45 ft cutter to a 14 ft boat, depending on the circumstances of his service. Pilot boats had one thing in common. Because the pilot's services were likely to be needed at any time the pilot vessel had to be very seaworthy in relation to the conditions prevailing in the area in which she worked.

When they came on the market after the First World War on the abandonment of sail in the pilotage service a number of them were taken up by yachtsmen, so that the Bristol Channel pilot cutter is the best-remembered of pilot vessels today. They were perhaps the finest for their purpose to be met with in British waters, but there were many more types of sailing pilot vessels in service.

74 *Humber Golddusters Racing*

These boats were used for pilotage and other work in and off the Humber. They were strong, burdensome, clinker-built boats, 16 to 18ft long, rigged with two masts of approximately the same height, from each of which was set a tall, narrow spritsail. This double-spritsail version of the shallop rig was much used in Europe and North America in the seventeenth and eighteenth centuries and on into the first part of the nineteenth century. At Pill in Somerset, at Liverpool and in the Channel Islands, three-masted boats rigged with spritsails on each mast were in use. Given a big crew such rigs were very flexible. The short masts could be stowed inside the boat and the sails could rapidly be changed around by re-stepping the masts to give various distributions of canvas to suit the prevailing conditions. The golddusters, for example, would go about under foresail alone.

Only on the Humber did the seventeenth-century two-masted sprit rig survive into the twentieth century in Britain. These golddusters were photographed racing at Hull City Regatta.

75 The Bristol Channel Pilot Cutter A Bristol Channel pilot cutter photographed in the 1890s. The cruising ground of some of these Bristol Channel pilots was between Scilly and the south of Ireland; others would go even further afield while some stayed within the Bristol Channel itself. In the main their seeking grounds were open to the North Atlantic gales and, particularly in the Bristol Channel, greatly affected by tides which with the wind against them could produce a vicious sea. The livelihood of the pilots depended on lying out until they met a vessel—often in later years by pre-arrangement—inward bound for one of the Bristol Channel ports. Then the pilot would tranship to the big vessel in a boat which was carried on the cutter's deck.

After the beginning of this century cutters from Pill in Somerset carried two pilots and two hands to sail the cutter. When both pilots had been placed on inward-bound ships the cutter either sailed back after them or, if the pilots had already arranged to take outward-bound vessels, the cutter went into Ilfracombe or Appledore to provision and water, and it is not surprising that Pill men married women from these places. The time on station was usually ten days to a fortnight and the cutter's great virtue was her ability to remain at sea in any weather for this period of time without exhausting those on board her. Cutters were not fast and they were wet when driven to windward, but they were usually safe and comfortable.

In the nineteenth century the pilot's life could be a hit and miss kind of existence, dependent on good fortune in meeting inward-bound shipping, but the Bristol Channel ports were prosperous and vessels frequent and on the whole the pilots were among the more highly paid of professional seamen. In the early twentieth century some earned the equivalent of a trans-Atlantic jet pilot's earnings today.

Cutters were built at Pill, Newport, Appledore and Looe in Cornwall among other places. It was said some years ago by a surviving sailing pilot of great experience that the best all-round cutters were those built at Portleven in Cornwall. One of these, the *Dolphin,* is still in commission as a yacht owned by George Naish, Keeper at the National Maritime Museum.

76 *The Swansea Pilot Schooners*

This remarkable photograph, taken about 1845 in Swansea, shows a totally different type of pilot vessel from the Bristol Channel cutters of a later date. These are the Swansea Bay pilot schooners, beautiful half-decked boats with the masts and sails of a seventeenth-century shallop or two-mast boat developed into a small schooner by the addition of a headsail set from a running bowsprit. The rake of the mainmast is markedly greater than that of the fore, the gaffs are very short, the standing rigging the simplest possible, the mainmast is stepped more or less amidships, the foremast right forward.

Swansea harbour in the eighteenth and early nineteenth centuries was tidal and it faces south-west. During periods of persistent south-west winds the harbour could become packed with vessels seeking shelter and it was in these conditions that the pilot boats were active. Pilots were put on board straight from the boats and in the course of the operation it was essential that the sails should be handled easily while alongside and hoisted quickly for sheering off. It was also essential that the masts should be short so as not to foul the yards of a square-rigged vessel and this precluded a tall cutter rig. The shallop rig which was widely used in the eighteenth century both in Europe and America seems to have met these requirements, and it was adopted by the Swansea pilots. At the end of the eighteenth century the boats were clinker-built, 21 ft long by local regulation and rigged as shallops without a headsail. The bowsprit and jib which made them into small schooners was adopted in the mid-nineteenth century as the range of operation of the pilots grew and their vessels were slowly increased in size. This photograph is of particular interest in that it was taken at this transitional time and the vessels it shows are between the clinker-built open boats of the eighteenth century and the large decked vessels which followed.

The Swansea pilot schooner in her larger and more developed form dropped out of use at the end of the nineteenth century.

77 *The Cornish Pilot Gig*

Among the most beautiful of British working boats was the Cornish version of the rowing gig—long, narrow, shallow, light, fast under oars, yet extremely seaworthy. In the Scilly Isles these gigs were used for putting pilots on board vessels seeking shelter among the islands and they were also used as rescue boats in extremely rough seas. Developed for rowing, they were never intended to sail, though a steadying mizzen was set (as in this photograph) and a dipping lug was sometimes used to take them to leeward.

The most famous gig builders were the Peters family of St Mawes who were responsible for the construction of some of the finest of these boats. Largely as a result of the efforts of one man, Richard Gillis of Newquay, Cornwall, interest in the gig has grown in recent years to the point at which a number of derelict gigs have been restored, at least one new one built, and gig racing under oars has been revived to become a thriving sport. Among the very old gigs in service today is the *Newquay*, built by the Peters family in 1812.

This working gig is the *Slippen*, built by the Peters about 1830, still in use in excellent condition in the late 1960s, photographed with her crew in 1907 when she was about to set out to recover bodies from the wreck of the great American schooner, the *Thomas W. Lawson*, lost among the islands a day or two before.

THE SAILING VESSEL IN PORT

In the later days of the sailing ship Britain's great ports presented a totally-different aspect from that familiar today. The first thing to be seen as you approached docks were the literally towering spars of the big steel barques and ships and the occasional big North American schooner. Around them, like a newer growth of timber, were the riggings of smaller square-rigged vessels and British schooners; bowsprits stretched over the wharves and figureheads peered into the doors of the warehouses. The pervading smells were of horses and tarred ropes, and small steam shunting engines puffed along the wharves and added their character-istic smells and noises. In a big dock system the towering masts stretched away into the distance in basin after basin. In total they supported many acres of canvas controlled by hundreds of miles of rope.

78 and 79 Swansea in the Early 1840s The two photographs of Swansea in the days when the harbour still dried out on almost every tide show a very different world from that of the last great steel merchant sailing ships and one more typical of the sailing ship in her long unchallenged years as a tool of expanding commerce in the eighteenth and early nineteenth centuries. These wooden full-rigged ships and barques, deep, flat-floored, full-bowed, sitting bolt upright on the mud, their stern cabins illuminated by windows in the transom counter, the great single topsails stowed in the bunt (ie, with the great bulk of the canvas bunched in the middle of the yard), their jibbooms and martingales, their shrouds set up from channels (narrow platforms outside the bulwarks) are representative of the greater number of merchant sailing vessels until the later years of the nineteenth century. These are the vessels which were served by the Swansea pilot schooners when they were still open boats and helped into harbour by paddle tugs which were the harbingers of a different age. One of these vessels, the left-hand one in the first photograph, has been identified as the full-rigged ship *Mary Dugdale*, built at Hull in 1835, 375 tons. The majority of them were employed in the copper ore trade around Cape Horn.

80 Swansea in the Middle 1890s   By way of contrast is this photograph of Prince of Wales Dock, Swansea, on 31 May 1894. This photograph and Plates 78 and 79 are separated by an economic and technical revolution which is reflected in different ways in almost every detail visible in them. The docks are unrecognisable, the vessels have altered to the last great steel sailing ships and to steamers. The two big sailing vessels in the foreground are the iron four-masted full-rigged ship *Falls of Foyers* of over 2,000 tons built in 1883 at Greenock, and the steel barque *Inverlyon* built ten years later at Port Glasgow, and therefore almost new when the photograph was taken.

81 Salthouse Dock, Liverpool in 1897   This photograph shows five large sailing vessels in the foreground and many more in the distance. The five are from left to right, the full-rigged ship *Wellington*, loading for Wellington and Dunedin in New Zealand, an unknown full-rigged ship laid up for sale, the four-masted ship *Highfields*, the Russian three-masted schooner *Zeriba*, and the Dutch steel barquentine *Zwijger*. (Illustration on facing page, below.)

82 The Alaska Packers Fleet in Oakland Creek, California   The only large fleet of square-rigged merchant sailing vessels in North America to survive into the second quarter of the twentieth century was that of the Alaska Packers Association of San Francisco. This fleet, comprising a collection of old wooden and steel barques, four-masted barques and full-rigged ships, with some barquentines, was employed in the seasonal trade of the Alaska salmon fishery. Their job was simply to take men and canning equipment north in the spring and return loaded with canned fish in the fall. For the greater part of the year they lay inactive, either in Oakland Creek, where more than a dozen of them are shown here as late as 1923, or in Alaskan waters. For such a trade old sailing vessels bought very cheaply and requiring small basic crews were the obvious vehicle as long as they could be manned and maintained economically. The fleet died out when these considerations ceased to apply in the late 1920s and early 30s, but the late survival of these vessels has resulted in the preservation of two of them as museum ships in California. One of these, the *Star of India*, formerly the *Euterpe*, is a vessel of especial historical interest in that she is an iron vessel, built at Ramsey, Isle of Man in 1863 as a passenger ship to operate between Britain and Australia.

THE FIGUREHEAD

The figurehead was a conspicious feature of many sailing vessels and one which was likely to be particularly interesting to the casual viewer of vessels at the dockside. They varied from ambitious pieces of portrait sculpture, sometimes of very considerable size, to simple carvings, primitives which were often both amusing and attractive. Where a vessel was named for a person the figurehead frequently represented him or her; often, whatever the name, they were portraits of someone connected with the vessel. In colour they varied from a uniform white to full gaudy colours of the fairground type. Many vessels had no figurehead in the strict sense of the term but a design of foliage and other carvings at the stemhead which was brought to its conclusion in a scroll device shaped like an uncoiling fern, as is the head of a violin. This was appropriately called a 'fiddle head'.

83 A Female Figurehead of the 1860s
The iron barque *Borrowdale* was built at Liverpool in 1868.

84 A Male Figurehead of the 1880s

This figurehead was, within the conventions of the period,
linked in subject and treatment to the name of the vessel
which carried it, the barque *Cambrian Chieftain*, built at
Sunderland in 1885.

85 A Female Figurehead of a Small Vessel of

the 1900s   The unknown woman who was the model
for the figurehead of the wooden ketch
Sunshine, built at Falmouth in 1900 by the Burt family, is
depicted in contemporary dress. This was quite a sophisticated
piece of sculpture for the figurehead of a small vessel.

WHEN SMALL HARBOURS WERE FILLED WITH SHIPPING

During much of the nineteenth century there was a steadily increasing demand for small ships to carry cargoes all over the world. When goods were made slowly in small quantities before the economies of large-scale production became apparent both raw materials and finished products changed hands in much smaller parcels than they do today. Small production units were widely scattered. Goods which were carried by sea tended to come in a small vessel to the seaport nearest the consumer and to be delivered from there, rather than to be shipped as part cargo to a great port from which they were transported by road or rail.

This was the age of the small business, the small cargo, the small vessel and the small harbour. Seaside places few people today would associate with commercial shipping were teeming with activity, with sailing vessels coming and going on every tide, their masts forming a spinney of tall timber towering over the waterside cottages. The vessels and the industries which they served and which served them, helped to set the tone of local life and the flavour of the community.

Britain today has many abandoned harbours. At many of them there are clear indications to the industrial archaeologist of their former activity and importance. Some are silted up, some partly washed away, some embedded in later urban developments or used only in the service of the tourist industry or for pleasure sailing.

86 Lochranza, Island of Arran

The small islands and other outlying communities of Scotland were dependent on sea transport for their existence. Trading smacks were grounded on the beach between tides and discharged their cargo into carts. Here coal is being winched out from the smack *Fairy Dell,* a vessel of most attractive shape.

87 *Portmadoc in the 1890s*

Portmadoc, later an abandoned harbour, was built in the 1820s to provide facilities for the export of local slate. The new town prospered, shipbuilding yards were established, and an extensive shipowning industry grew up. The local vessels began to be taken up for cargoes which took them all over the world and by the 1870s square-rigged sailing ships and schooners lay in the port loading, discharging and repairing in dozens. Portmadoc shipowners with their big three-masted schooners dominated the later years of the historic Newfoundland trade with Britain. The building of wooden sailing ships at Portmadoc continued until the First World War. Twenty-seven sailing vessels are visible in this photograph taken in the 1890s and two more are in frame on the slope facing the camera across the channel in the foreground.

88 *Bridgwater River, Somerset*

Small wooden barques carried cargoes everywhere. There is no modern equivalent of the sort of business they did, carrying a few hundred tons of goods at a time anywhere in the world, but often loading or discharging it at one of the smaller centres, or somewhere where there was no harbour at all.

This Swedish wooden barque, the *Biland*, discharging cargo into a Severn trow in the estuary of the Bridgwater river, began life as the *Prince Rupert*, built at Sunderland by John Briggs in 1865 and bought, while she was being built, by the Hudson Bay Company. She sailed annually from London to York Factory on the west coast of Hudson's Bay with supplies, returning with fur, then she made eight voyages from England to Victoria, British Columbia, each of which involved the double rounding of Cape Horn. She arrived back from the last of these voyages in March 1886 and was sold next month to Scandinavian owners.

89 and 90 Appledore, Devon

A number of references have already been made in this book to the small town of Appledore in North Devon. A thriving shipping centre in the nineteenth century with a considerable trade with Canada, a large shipbuilding industry for its size and population and a very extensive fleet of locally-owned vessels employed in the home trade, its people comprised one of the most vigorous and enterprising seafaring communities in western Britain. The commercial operation of boats and vessels with sails lasted longest at Appledore and, incredible though it may seem, it was not until 1960 that the last schooner and the last ketch ceased to operate commercially from the town.

The first of these two photographs was taken in the early 1870s and it shows a dozen vessels off the Appledore waterfront. Alongside the quay is the trading smack *Happy Return* built at Fowey in 1846, and in the centre of the picture is the polacca brigantine *Newton*, built at Cleave Houses near Bideford in 1788 by Richard Chapman.

The second photograph was taken in the early years of this century. It shows the old quay, completed in 1844 and just wide enough for a four-wheeled cart to turn on it. More than a dozen vessels are in the river; the *Rosamund Jane* in the foreground was one of the last of the smacks. The boys appear to be exchanging boyish compliments. The lad with the sack follows the local custom, persistent well into the twentieth century, of going bare foot when out of school.

In the last century, despite the prosperity of some members of the community, the life of many of the men and women of the place was very poor and hard. In the vivid local phraseology they had to 'work for their breakfast before they could eat it'. No wonder the town was noted for the lawlessness of some of its people as for its own strong local dialect, which extended to cover even technical terms used at sea.

91 Three Smacks Lying in Porth Gaverne   No photograph we have examined
has conveyed to us as vividly as this
one does the simplicity of much local sea transport in the nineteenth century. Three smacks
lie on the sands at Porth Gaverne in north Cornwall, loading and discharging cargo brought
and taken away in carts. This little crack in the rocks served an extensive area without railways and with very poor roads. There were many such coves and beaches rating as harbours

for local areas all round the coasts of Britain. The small local industries, the farms and villages were dependent on them for their coal, timber, many finished goods and for the transport away of the products of local quarries, mines, and much agricultural produce. Much of the slate from the great Delabole quarries went out from Porth Gaverne in smacks like these. At an earlier period the slates were carried down from the quarries in wagons pulled by six oxen led by a horse.

92 *Littlehampton*

Littlehampton became a port in its own right only in 1869, but in the later years of the century it was a busy centre of shipping business and shipbuilding. A Littlehampton vessel, the *Robert and Mary*, was the last British brig to visit Cape Town. Henry Harvey and his successors, J. & W. B. Harvey, the local shipbuilders, were in business on a relatively large scale and the square-rigged vessels they built sailed all over the world. Their last merchant sailing vessel, the ketch *Moultonian*, was built as late as 1919.

In this photograph of Littlehampton the brigantine is called the *Adela*. The owner of the ketch-rigged yacht *Wanderer* in the foreground belonged to the Royal Yacht Squadron. The London river barge is the *Viking* of Rochester and alongside her is what is evidently an early petrol-driven launch, the *Wigeon*. The brig is the *Sarah* of Shoreham, built at Shoreham in 1862 and launched by Miss Sarah Banfield, a daughter of the owner, after whom the vessel was named. The figurehead, clearly visible in the original photograph, depicts Miss Banfield herself. The *Sarah* was in the coal trade, bringing cargoes to Shoreham and later to Littlehampton (where she was owned from 1895 to 1910) from Hartlepool and other north-east coast ports.

93 *Whitby, Yorkshire*   Whitby, a famous port in the home and Baltic trades and in the whaling industry in the eighteenth and nineteenth centuries, notable particularly as the home port of Captain James Cook in his early years at sea, is shown busy with shipping. The ketches *Lively, Sarah* and *Hopewell* are lying on the left-hand side of the picture with a brig behind them and cobles (see Plate 122) are drying their sails. In the foreground is the schooner *Alert,* built at Whitby in 1802.

THE MERCHANT SCHOONERS

The schooner rig, in which the greater part of the working canvas was always set fore-and-aft, was developed from Dutch and British models in the American colonies in the eighteenth century. During the nineteenth century it was gradually adopted in Britain, at first in ports with trades to which it was particularly suited and in ports with close contacts with North America. After 1870 the schooner became the typical small British merchant sailing ship and was to be found all over the world where there were small cargoes to be carried.

In particular, British schooners were engaged in large numbers in the hard trade across the North Atlantic to Newfoundland and back to Europe with cargoes of salted cod fish. Many schooners were built in Prince Edward Island, Canada, for British owners. Hundreds were launched all around the shores of Britain, though the schooner was always particularly associated with the smaller harbours of western, and particularly south-western England.

The schooner was developed in New England and the maritime provinces of Canada in several different directions. Thousands of small two-masted schooners with particularly graceful low hulls with sweeping sheer, tall lower masts and usually no foretopmast, were built for the coasting trade. Many of them had drop keels like modern racing dinghies and many big yachts in the United States today. Larger and larger schooner-rigged vessels were built and the middle-sized schooners, the three- and four-masters (plate 14) grew to a high degree of efficiency.

94 A Schooner of the 1840s It was in the 1840s that the schooner appears to have begun to come into large-scale use in Britain as a small merchant sailing ship. This photograph, taken in South Wales in the 1840s, is the earliest known of a British schooner. She is very sharp, with marked rise of floor, and it is possible that she is an early Prince Edward Island-built schooner.

95 *A Typical Small North American Merchant Schooner* This vessel is the *Ella*, built in 1869 by John H. Abeal at Northport, Long Island, New York for C. F. Sammis. She was 70 ft long and constructed of oak and chestnut with iron fastenings. Her cargoes in the coasting trade included cord wood, sand, bricks, tiles, oysters and oyster shells. Her extremely graceful shape is typical of many of the small American merchant schooners which, with their tall masts, were among the most attractive small sailing vessels ever to be developed. Many of them, with beamy shallow hulls were fast and able in the waters in which they worked. They were an essential part of the New England coastal scene until recent years, and because replicas of them are being built as yachts today and other schooners have been restored or built for the pleasure sailing business in Penobscot Bay, it is still possible to see vessels of traditional merchant schooner appearance sailing among the pine tree covered islands of the Maine coast.

96 *The Canadian Tern Schooner*

The typical larger schooner of Nova Scotia was the 'tern' with her three masts of the same height—the term 'tern' is probably derived from an expression used in poker meaning 'three of a kind' and it continued in use until the last tern schooner ceased to trade in the late 1940s. The first Nova Scotia tern was built in 1858, the last one, the *Mary B. Brooks* was completed in 1926. A fleet of them was sailing regularly backwards and forwards across the North Atlantic until far into World War II. Of one of these later Canadian terns the nautical historian Sir Alan Moore wrote in *The Last Days of Mast and Sail*: 'One of the most beautiful vessels I have ever seen sailed into the bay, rounded to in her own length almost, and began to shorten sail. She was a Nova Scotiaman, the three-masted fore-and-aft schooner *Frances Louise* (built at Lunenburg in 1917). She had a low, graceful hull painted black, a yacht-like counter, and a rounded cut away stem. Her masts raked slightly, and the mizzen mast was the tallest. . . . All her canvas was beautifully cut. She seemed the last word in sail. . . .'

Plate 96 shows the *Marion G. Douglas,* 449 tons net, built, also in 1917, at Fox River, at the end of a difficult passage across the North Atlantic during which she sustained weather damage and was abandoned by her crew. The derelict was picked up and brought into the Scilly Isles. Here she is towing a Scilly Pilot gig, like that shown in Plate 77.

97 *The Four-masted Schooner Joseph B. Thomas*

The *Joseph B. Thomas* was built at Thomaston, Maine, in 1900. She is typical of the best type of big New England-built schooner and in general appearance very like the vessel illustrated in Plate 14. This photograph shows her outward bound from Bristol, England on a return voyage across the North Atlantic. She is being towed down the river Avon and is passing a P. & A. Campbell pleasure steamer and a Westcountry ketch. This splendid deck view conveys an excellent impression of the simplicity of the rigging and fittings of one of these last great wooden merchant sailing ships. Her houses are half sunk into the deck, her rail is low and open, her long open deck uncluttered with gear, her rigging extremely simple, her towering masts almost awe-inspiring in their naked straightness.

98 A Schooner of the 1870s The *Ocean Wave* was built at Appledore in 1870 by
Thomas Peter Cook, whose yard was on the south side
of the present Richmond dry-dock. Owned in Fowey, she was in the Mediterranean and
Newfoundland trades from Britain and she was an excellent example of the big two-masted
Westcountry schooner of the 70s. A vessel of this size—she was 100 ft long—if she had been
built a few years later would have been three-masted. She was lost, missing without trace, in
1914.

99 A Schooner of the Twentieth Century The *John Llewelyn* was built in
Portmadoc, Caernarvonshire in 1904
and she represents the final development of the small deep-sea merchant sailing vessel in
Britain. She has a bold sheer and a strong seaworthy hull and a great deal of square canvas
on her foremast. Lying in St John's, Newfoundland, she can be seen to differ completely from
the typical North American three-masted schooner behind her. This vessel is considerably
bigger, has no square canvas, her masts are all the same height and some of her sails and
rigging probably interchangeable.

100   A Great Five-Master   This is the *Dunham Wheeler* of New York, a typical five-master built by the famous schooner-building firm of Percy & Small at Bath, Maine in 1917, one of the many great schooners built in the United States in the present century. She was lost off Cape Kennedy in 1930.

Dunham Wheeler, like nearly all other big North American schooners, was built of wood. She had no bulwarks but an open rail all round. Her hands lived in a deck house aft. She probably had central heating, certainly she was dependent on steam-power to handle the huge sails. She probably had a deck telephone system. The gaff and boomsails on the first four masts and many items of the gear throughout the rigging were interchangeable. She could be handled by a far smaller crew than any other vessel of her size, sail or power. Built of local materials, locally financed, representing a smaller capital investment than any other type of vessel of her size, very efficient for the classes of cargoes, the routes and the port facilities for which she was designed, the *Dunham Wheeler* and scores of vessels like her represent in some ways the high tide, as they do the last tide, in the long history of the development of the commercial sailing ship. Principally engaged in the long-range coastal trade of eastern North America, she crossed the Atlantic to Britain at least once.

FOUR NORTH AMERICAN SAILING VESSELS

It has already been said that the schooner rig was developed in the North American colonies in the eighteenth century; in the last section some examples of its later development in Britain and North America were illustrated. Besides these merchant vessels, smaller schooners employed in the North Atlantic fishing industry from Boston, Gloucester, Lunenburg and down Maine were developed out of recognition into one of the finest and most efficient types of commercial sailing vessel ever built.

Alongside the development of the schooner to its finest forms, there went on existing in North America, as everyday working craft, very early forms of the schooner, long after they had ceased to be seen in Europe. Two of these simple kinds of schooner have lasted into the mid-twentieth century and are the last working sailing vessels in use in North America. Examples of them are shown here.

101 The Pin Flat
The pin flat, pinne or bateau plat operated on the upper St Lawrence between Quebec City and Montreal and vessels of this type continued to earn a living until the 1920s when diesel engines replaced the sails. Her rig is like that of a seventeenth-century ketch and may well be directly descended from that period, with changes over the years to suit the river environment. Pin flats carried all the produce of the river, but especially timber, as their successors, the motor 'goelettes' do today.

102 The Gaspé Schooner
One of the roots from which the various forms of schooner developed in the seventeenth and eighteenth centuries was the shallop, or two-mast boat. This was a boat or small vessel with two masts, the mainmast stepped about amidships and the foremast in the bows, from which were set, latterly, two gaff or sprit or triangular sails. The addition of a headsail made her a small schooner. This sail plan was very widely used on both sides of the Atlantic until the mid-nineteenth century, after which it rapidly died out.

Small schooners which represent the first stage of development of the schooner from the shallop are still in use as fishing vessels on the southern coast of the Gaspé Peninsula in

Quebec Province, Canada. They differ little from the fishing vessels known to have been used on the coast of Massachusetts about the time of the American Revolution. Their shape is remarkably similar to that of the *Peggy*, the small eighteenth-century schooner preserved at the Maritime Museum at Castletown, Isle of Man.

Here the crew of one of these Gaspé schooners is line fishing from the vessel herself, the method used by New England and Canadian fishermen before the introduction in 1858 of the dory fishing described by Kipling in *Captains Courageous*.

103 The Sanxton Hubbard of Cambridge, Maryland

So far not one single photograph in this book has shown a vessel which worked for her living equipped with the three-cornered Bermudan sail which the modern British pleasure-sailing craft, whatever her size, wears almost like a uniform. The reason is simply that in the age of the camera only at two or three places in the world did working vessels of any size use the jib-headed sail because for a variety of reasons it was suitable for working craft only under very special conditions. One of these places was, and still is today, Chesapeake Bay.

Here a great fleet of Bermudan sloops, schooners and ketches (though they are never described as such but dubbed by their hull construction, skipjacks and bugeyes) were employed in the local oyster fishery. Laws forbidding oyster-dredging under power are still in force and the bugeyes and skipjacks still at work comprise one of the last working sailing fleets in the western world.

Sanxton Hubbard, a typical small bugeye, the sailplan of which is that of a simple schooner with jib-headed sails, was built at Solomons, Maryland, in 1891.

104 *Captains Courageous— the North American Fishing Schooner*

The cod-fishing industry on the shallow banks off the coast of New England, Nova Scotia, Newfoundland and in the Gulf of St Lawrence has been established since the fifteenth century. For much of the intervening period it has constituted an important economic and political factor in the history of the nations engaged in it. In the age of the camera the fishery was conducted by, among other sailing vessels, United States and Canadian schooners whose crews fished at first from the open decks. Then in the 1850s the technique was developed of extending a schooner's fishing area by carrying mass-produced, flat-bottomed boats, dories, which were dropped over the side with one or two men on board who rowed some distance from the schooner. This is the kind of fishing so graphically and accurately described in Rudyard Kipling's *Captains Courageous,* and so well illustrated in the old film of that story which is still a popular favourite.

At the end of the century, a new type of very powerful and fast fishing schooner was developed which became one of the finest types of commercial sailing vessel. Two of these later fishing schooners are here seen at one of the International Fishermen's races held between Canadian and United States vessels. The vessel nearest the camera is the Canadian *Bluenose* of which a full-sized sailing replica has recently been built. Readers familiar with the gaff rig will note with interest the way in which the efficiency of the *Bluenose's* gaff topsails is increased by threading them through between peak halyard and gaff. Water-colours of west of England schooners of the 1860s and 70s show that this method of setting the gaff topsail was widely used in Britain at that period.

SAILING BARGES

The different kinds of local cargo vessels which were called sailing barges in Britain were in many cases the end product of a process of evolution by which a river craft gradually developed into an efficient carrier in the conditions applying in a limited area of open water, as well as in the river where she began. This statement is not universally true. The larger Westcountry sailing barges had some of the coasting smack in their ancestry. But it certainly applies to the two kinds of sailing barge which developed furthest, the London river barge and the Severn trow, seagoing vessels in the late nineteenth century the origins of which can be traced back to river craft not so very long before.

The considerable interest of the different varieties of sailing barge, each adapted to be an efficient instrument in the waters and economic conditions in which they plied, is now widely recognised. The London river barge in particular has attracted attention because it was still to be found at work relatively recently in the area of greatest concentration of population in Britain. A number of these barges are still in use as pleasure vessels and at the time of writing two, the *Cambria* and the *May*, are still trading.

Besides their interest as specialised tools of man, most sailing barges were very handsome vessels when under sail, the London river barges particularly so. Less obviously, many sailing barges had hulls of considerable beauty. The Westcountry vessels had well-shaped burdensome hulls often with a fine run. The Severn trows with round full bows and steep sheer were among the most attractive local vessels to be seen around the British coasts.

105 *The London River Barge (i)*

The London river sailing barge was the great maid-of-all-work in the transport business of later nineteenth and early twentieth-century south-eastern Britain. She carried every kind of cargo generated by the metropolis and the towns and agricultural areas to the east of it. There were thousands of sailing barges on the Thames and the adjoining coasts and they were very

much a part of the life of London and the south and east coast ports. Latterly they sailed far and wide and the bigger barges have operated between the Tyne and the Bristol Channel.

Some nineteenth-century barges, like this one seen leading a wooden barque and a schooner down-river past Cubitt Town, were scow-shaped or 'swim headed' in the bows, as the earliest sailing barges had been. Very clearly shown in this photograph is the Thames barge's distinctive spritsail rig, a large and more complicated version of the rig of the sprit-rigged boats already described (see Plates 17 and 74). The Thames barges were the largest vessels to be rigged with spritsails in the age of the camera. All depended on lee-boards which were lowered when sailing to windward. These lee-boards fulfilled the function of the centre-plate in a modern sailing dinghy.

106 *The London River Barge (ii)*

The London river sailing barge developed a great deal during the age of the camera. These twentieth-century barges photographed off Greenwich in the 1930s are bigger than that shown in the first photograph. They have round bows and straight stems. Their mizzen masts are stepped well inboard instead of on the rudderhead and their mainsails and topsails are taller and of more efficient shape than those of the earlier barges. These sails were usually tanned indian-red. In some cases, as with the barge in the foreground, opportunity was taken to advertise the business of the vessel's owners or that of others willing to pay for the space.

107 *The London River Barge (iii)* The London river sailing barges developed in one direction into a specialised trading ketch with leeboards to enable her to sail to windward but with a hull which above the waterline had the appearance of a Westcountry merchant ketch with a ketch's gaff and boom-sails. The *Cock of the Walk*, built at Millwall, was one of these ketch barges, as they were called. She was built in 1876 and lost during the First World War. Like her sister ketch barges she competed in the general home trade, though most of her work was done to and from the shallow harbours of the east coast and the Netherlands. On her stern were carved the words 'While I live I Crow'.

108 *The Westcountry Sailing Barge (i)*

The *Lillie* was built by James Goss at Bere Alston in 1899 (see Plate 24).

The sailing barges which served on the rivers and coasts of southwest England could be divided into two broad categories, inside barges and outside barges. The inside barges sailed on the rivers and their estuaries, particularly on the Tamar, the Fal, the Camel, the Taw and the Torridge. The outside barges sailed on the rivers

and also around the coasts from one river to another.

There were great variations among these barges, but in general those from the same rivers tended to resemble one another closely. They were built by local builders to operate in the same conditions. Almost all were cutter-rigged, though often referred to by their men as sloops, with gaff and boomsails. Some had gaff topsails. The barges of the Camel, unique in Britain, were small fore-and-aft schooners.

A bargeman had a pleasant, if hard-working, life. He worked in surroundings of great natural beauty and he often slept at home. The largest number of barges was on the Tamar, which with its heavily-industrialised banks was alive with traffic in the second half of the nineteenth century. The *Lillie* was built as an inside barge and later converted by the addition of higher bulwarks and hatch-coamings to be an outside barge. After conversion she used to take stone from the Lynher river as far as Portland. Notice the great iron hand-winch in front of the mast—this was used for working the cargo. Notice also the 'barge boat', an essential piece of equipment for river sailing, lying on the hatch. The two men in the photograph were probably the Taylors, father and son, who worked with the *Lillie* for years.

109 The Westcountry Sailing Barge (ii)

Whenever a local community was developing, with much building and construction work going forward, there was a demand for sand for concrete and mortar. When no cargoes were offering, the crews of Tamar barges would go out and dredge sand from the bed of the river to sell to the contractors working on construction projects in Devonport dockyard. A whole fleet of sailing barges spent much of their time collecting sand at low tide from the banks in the Torridge and the Taw in north Devon to be delivered on the following flood to contractors in Bideford, Barnstaple and Braunton. The photograph shows a group of these barges aground, their sails fluttering while their men sweat to load them with shovelfuls thrown from the sandbanks over the sides of the barges into their holds. It was taken in the early years of this century but the awful labour of loading the barges with shovels went on till the 1930s, though by then all the barges had motors.

110 The Severn Trow Of all the sailing barges of Britain the Severn trow was one of the most interesting. Her history has been recorded by the West of England maritime historian Grahame Farr. The true trow was completely open for the greater part of her length, the heaped-up cargo was covered with tarpaulins, and her bulwarks were extended upwards with canvas side-cloths, held up by metal stretchers. She was flat-bottomed without a keel, though of round-bilged construction. To sail to windward she used a movable keelboard, which was slung over the side with chains, in place of the centreboard which her American equivalent would have had built into her, or the leeboards of the London river barge or the Humber keel. Her stern was particularly full and she had a deep flat transom with the rudder outside it like that of an open boat.

True trows of this kind, sloop or ketch-rigged, sailed far up the river Severn and its tributaries and down its estuary and out into the Bristol Channel as far west as Milford Haven and the Cornish coast. In the 1890s for safety reasons they were prohibited from sailing west of the Somerset coast and vessels of the trow hull-form, but decked or partly-decked, took over the long-distance trades. Like the London river sailing barges the trows were used to take cargoes far beyond the waters for which they had been evolved. Decked trows traded between Glasgow and Holland.

This photograph shows the *Ark,* an open trow built at Framilode, Gloucestershire in 1871. She traded from Lydney and Cardiff to Bridgwater with coal and she is shown outward-bound, sailing light, down the river Parret with her master 'Tuggie' Warren at the wheel. Ahead of her is the Bridgwater ketch *Fanny Jane,* built at Bridgwater in 1858.

111 *The Norfolk Wherry*

The Norfolk wherry was a shallow, clinker-built boat about 50 ft long and perhaps 12 ft wide with short decks fore-and-aft separated by a great hatchway with very high coamings. She had a single mast well forward, from which was set a big loose-footed square-headed gaffsail. She had a single halyard to raise the long gaff and no boom. She had no shrouds, and her rig in fact was the simplest possible for a vessel of her size. Her mast could easily be lowered when a bridge had to be negotiated, and in the skilled hands of her crew she could maintain her way until it was raised and the sail set again.

The wherry developed in the eighteenth century from a smaller passenger and cargo vessel. During the nineteenth century, being admirably suited to conditions both economic and physical on the rivers and broads of Norfolk, she changed very little, and because of the development of the holiday boating industry on the broads she became one of the best-known types of local sailing vessel in Britain. But her position was more vulnerable than that of some other sailing barges and with changing economic conditions the wherries were already greatly reduced in numbers by the end of the nineteenth century. One wherry, the *Albion*, has been restored and kept sailing by a local trust, and because of this far-sighted act of preservation the wherry is one of the few types of vessel illustrated in this book which it is still possible to see under sail.

112 The River Ouse Barge This sprit-rigged barge on the river Ouse is bound for Lewes from Newhaven, Sussex. The photograph is included to show an example of one of the extremely simple types of vessel with simple rigging and sails which was used on a number of rivers in Britain before motor transport replaced them. Sailing barges of equal simplicity with masts easily lowered for going under bridges were operated on the rivers of Kent, the Bristol Avon, the Teign, the Mersey, the lakes of Westmorland, and in numerous other places where there was water enough to make a highway and where good roads in the country districts were few.

113 Humber Keels These keels were photographed at Thorne on the Stainforth & Keadby canal at the Sheffield & South Yorkshire Navigation's yard about the year 1900.

The term keel used to be used for square-rigged sailing barges of different kinds all the way from Norfolk to Northumberland; there were Norfolk keels and Tyne keels of widely differing hull form. These are Yorkshire keels which, in their turn, differed from one another at least in size, depending on the locks through which they customarily worked. Thus there were the Sheffield size, Barnsley size, and Driffield size. Yorkshire keels were massively built, very burdensome with full round bows and stern. The planks of the bows of some keels were so massive and the hull so near a rectangle in plan that Sir Alan Moore, the maritime historian, was moved in his remarkable book *The Last Days of Mast and Sail*, to comment that 'it is a wonder the planks can be so much bent'. With such a hull-form leeboards were essential for windward sailing, but in fact the keel in general was faced with an environment in which tides mattered more than wind. In her world there was little to be gained by sailing to windward, but winds abaft the beam could be made good use of. In these circumstances, as in similar conditions in East Pakistan and elsewhere in the world, the square sail persisted long after it was abandoned by sailing barges everywhere else. Despite their rig, like the London river barges and the Severn trows, the Yorkshire keels sailed far from their mother river and they even carried cargoes to London.

THE FISHING INDUSTRY UNDER SAIL

The nineteenth century was the great era of the sailing fishery in Britain. The demand for fish expanded with the improvement of communications on land and the increase in population; great fleets of sailing fishing vessels grew up and not until the later years of the century did the steam trawler become firmly established. In some places the sailing fishery lingered on until the 1930s.

Every beach, creek and river had its small fishing boats. Most seaside communities derived some of their income from the industry. Harbours like Brixham, Penzance, St Ives, Yarmouth, Lowestoft, Aberdeen, Peterhead and many more had great fleets of large vessels. In the early 1800s these were open boats, but they developed into powerful decked craft as the century advanced.

In the age of the camera almost every lug-rigged fishing vessel around the British Isles was two-masted like those in Plate 16. But in the eighteenth and early nineteenth centuries the ancestors of some luggers were three-masted. The third mast was abandoned because it and its sail got in the way of the fishing work and for most of the time the boats sailed as well without the third sail as with it.

The life of the poorer fisherman was very hard. These people were for the most part sea-faring peasants who went to sea because they had to, because there was no alternative way of living open to them in the environment into which they were born. A small cargo-carrying sailing vessel could, with luck, skill and industry, make a small fortune for her owners who often included her master and members of his family. A beach fisherman could never hope to make this sort of capital, he could not found a prosperous middle-class family on the earnings of a 15 ft boat or even a 22 ft lugger, though the latter might cost only £100 complete with all her gear.

A first-hand account of sailing and fishing in this type of boat, the economics of the industry and the domestic lives of the fishermen before the First World War is to be found in the writings of Stephen Reynolds, who lived among the fishermen of Sidmouth, Devon, for a number of years. He paints a picture of poverty and hardship which, by being instrumental in assisting with the introduction of motors, he was able to do something to alleviate.

114 *Clovelly* One of the most charming fishing places in Britain is the village of Clovelly, built down a steep cleft in high wooded cliffs. Today a very popular beauty spot, visited by thousands of people every year, Clovelly still has a small herring fishery. Once its people ground a hard, poor living from the sea. Clovelly Roads was a recognised sheltering place for smaller merchant vessels in an area, the western part of the Bristol Channel, where sheltering places are few.

Clovelly had its own type of fishing boat, the picarooners, 13 to 16 ft long, with a distinctive type of transom stern. They were introduced towards the end of the nineteenth century for the inshore fishery and were unusual for British beach boats in that some of them were half-decked. The picarooners were all built at Appledore and one of the last of them to survive, constructed in the 1890s, has recently been acquired by the National Maritime Museum to form part of a small display of examples of the world's working boats.

This photograph shows Clovelly fishermen in about the year 1880. The two old gentlemen on the right-hand side must have been survivors of the hard days of the 1830s and 40s and were perhaps born before Trafalgar.

115 and 116 Newlyn, Cornwall   Newlyn was one of the bases for west Cornish luggers. The vessels belonging there differed from the east Cornish vessels shown in Plate 16 chiefly in that they were 'double-ended', that is, they had pointed sterns instead of transoms. Newlyn was also always frequented by great numbers of foreign vessels, many of them from Brittany. which used it as a place of refreshment and refuge.

The first of these two photographs, taken at the end of the last century, shows potential buyers and casual onlookers inspecting fish as it is brought ashore from a vessel to be sold. A barquentine rigged down to her main and mizzen lower masts and foretopmast and yards, and a three-masted schooner lie further out in the harbour. In the street scene, a one-man band is entertaining children and women at an intersection of two of the little town's cobbled alleyways.

117 *Brixham Trawlers*

Brixham, in south Devon, was a very important harbour in the history of the British fishing industry. From at least the sixteenth century sailing craft from Brixham fished the North Sea. The harbour was much improved in the eighteenth century and by 1818 Brixham vessels were fishing anywhere from the Dogger Bank to Dublin Bay. In the middle of the nineteenth century Brixham was one of the most prosperous places on the shores of the English Channel; her fishing enterprise led to the establishment of the industry at many of the big North Sea ports.

By the end of the nineteenth century the Brixham trawler had developed into the largest and most powerful of British sailing fishing craft. Of the group of these vessels shown in this photograph DH 121 *Dauntless*, which is being caulked between tides, was built by Samuel Dewdney at Brixham in 1885. DH 407 *Roebuck* in the background was built, also at Brixham, by J. W. & A. Upham in 1896. The photograph was taken between that year and 1902 when the Dartmouth prefix DH was replaced by Brixham's BM.

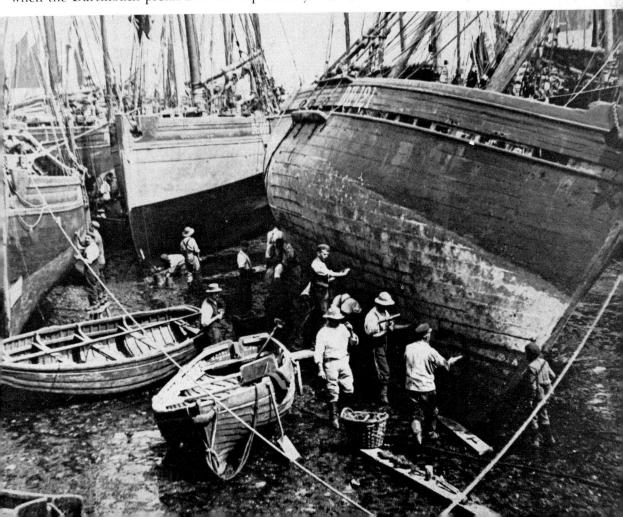

118 A South Coast Lug-and-Mizzen-rigged Boat

This beautiful 14 ft beach fishing boat is shown sailing under a big dipping lug foresail and a working lug mizzen. The dipping lug, though it had to be taken in every time the boat went about, a process which required much skill, was a powerful and handsome sail and a much better performer to windward than might be imagined. This boat is, in general appearance, typical of thousands which earned a living fishing around the coasts of Britain.

119 A Rochester Bawley

The bawley with its loose-footed mainsail and shallow, beamy, round-bilged hull was once a familiar sight on the lower Thames where she was used as a general-purpose fishing vessel. This bawley, the *Ethel*, was photographed near Southend in 1910.

120 *Lowestoft*   Like Brixham, Lowestoft was a great base for sailing trawlers which, when they were gathered together in harbour, provided visitors with an endlessly changing pattern of activity to watch. This photograph was probably taken in the 1890s and the vessel in the middle of the picture is a visitor, the ketch *Criterion* of Ramsgate.

121 *Lowestoft Fishermen*   Members of the 'Old Company of Lowestoft Beachmen' in their lookout about 1890. On the right is Robert Hook, locally famous for his service as lifeboat coxswain.

122 A Yorkshire Coble and her Men

The coble from the north-east coast of England was, and is, one of the most distinctive local working boats in Britain.

She was designed as a beach boat for launching into surf, and within the technical limitations of nineteenth-century beach fishing she met this purpose extremely well. Like most working boats of highly individual form she sailed and rowed very well in the hands of experts who earned their living with her, making her way to windward despite her flat run and the absence of a drop-keel because of her deep, sharp forefoot and long rudder. Suitably shortened down it was said that a sailing coble could survive almost any weather if kept by the wind. According to Warington Smyth in that splendid book *Mast and Sail in Europe and Asia,* a coble in bad weather was 'sailed by the sheet and never luffs to the stiffest puffs'.

With her sharp high bow and very flat sections in the stern, the coble anticipated modern motorboat practice by many years. In some ways she slightly resembles in form some of the modern North American lobster boats which have been developed from the Nova Scotian Cape Islander model. Like them she was, and is, a very large open boat running up to 35 or 40 ft in length.

The clinker-built coble was normally equipped with a tall, narrow dipping lug and she was rowed with oars equipped with an iron ring which set over a single thole-pin. Today motor cobles by the score are still at work, of length from 14 ft upwards.

123 A Herring Fleet at Scarborough, Yorkshire 22 September 1897

Scenes like this must have been the origin of the expression 'a forest of masts'. One of the authors has seen cargo-carrying sailing boats on the rivers of East Pakistan in similar profusion, but nothing like this has been seen in the western world for half a century. The bathing machines help to set the social scene. The solitary brigantine seems trapped in the surrounding host of ketches.

124 A Lerwick Ketch

Here is a close-up of one of the ketches of the great fleet. She is being hauled into a wharfside by her crew. Notice the running bowsprit, run in, and the iron traveller-ring on which the tack of the jib was hauled out when the sail was set.

THE TALL SHIPS PASS

The use of sailing vessels for transport and fishing began to decline in the second half of the nineteenth century. The decline was at first relative, industrial activity was expanding, world demand was rising, more sailing vessels were being built. But because of the changing scale of industry, the development of communications, technical changes in business methods and the improvement of powered vessels, the curve of growth of the western world's sailing fleets began to flatten out, then to turn downwards.

The first to go were the inefficient units, the small wooden barques and brigs which had carried so much of the world's cargoes, but which were expensive to build and run in relation to their earning power. The sailing vessel continued to develop in the later nineteenth century. In Britain the great steel four-masted barques were built which could offer reasonably regular, low-cost, bulk transport of big cargoes. The Germans carried the development of this type of vessel even further in the early twentieth century. The huge North American schooners with their small crews were highly competitive in some trades. The much smaller British schooners and the ketches continued to be built in considerable numbers to carry some of the remaining small cargoes on deep water and to operate in the British home trade.

After 1900 few commercial sailing vessels, except for large North American schooners, were built. Nevertheless they were a very long time dying out of use. The large square-rigged sailing ship ceased to be a serious factor in ocean transport after the First World War, the big schooners lasted somewhat longer in the North American coasting trade. The last British sailing fishing fleets died out finally in the 1930s, but one, the oyster-dredging fleet which works in Carrick Roadstead in south Cornwall, like the Maryland oyster dredgers in the United States, still survives as a miniature working fleet, and at the time of writing it is actually increasing in numbers and new sailing fishing boats are being built for the business. The merchant schooners and London river and Westcountry sailing barges lingered on in relatively large numbers in the British home trade until the Second World War and a few of them went on working until the 1960s. Thus it is true that in Britain the commercial sailing vessel survived into the space age.

125 The Loss of the Ardencraig

Sailing vessels ended their lives in various ways; the most dramatic of course were sinking at sea and shipwreck on a storm-bound coast. This photograph shows the full-rigged ship *Ardencraig*, built in 1886, sinking off the Scilly Isles in January 1911.

126 *A Vessel Ashore*

The ketch *Elizabeth*, like many other vessels, had painted on her stern the name both of the town in which she was owned and of the port of which the town was legally a part—in her case 'Bude - Port of Bideford'. It was at Bude she ended her days, thrown high up on the rocks under Summerlease Point in February 1912. A wreck was always an object of curious attention when the sea had died down. It was something out of the ordinary to visit and talk about. Here men and women of different classes and ages have come to view the shattered vessel.

127 *A Vessel being Broken Up*

This is the schooner *Annie Christian*, later named *Ade* and ketch-rigged, being broken up at Appledore in 1950. Iron and steel sailing ships made profitable scrap, but wooden vessels, far more difficult to break up, were often slowly dismantled by men who scraped a living from selling the copper of the fastenings or the wood for gateposts, rafters, door-lintels and firewood. Many of the older houses in small harbour towns have vessel-timber in their construction.

The *Annie Christian's* massive build is clearly revealed in this photograph. Launched at Barnstaple by J. Westacott, it is little wonder that she survived sixty-five years of working life.

ACKNOWLEDGMENTS

(a) Photographs of which the National Maritime Museum has charge: W. G. M. Edwards, Plate 1; Nautical Photo Agency Coll, 2, 3, 4, 5, 6, 10, 12, 31, 35, 36, 45, 46, 47, 48, 52, 55, 61, 62, 63, 65, 74, 75, 82, 101, 118; R. Morton Nance, 16; Fox Coll, 17, 18, 51, 90, 109, 115, 116, 117; Fraser Coll, 23; L. W. Moore, 25; W. A. Sharman, 28, 37, 83, 84, 85, 88, 110; J. Richards, Polruan, 29; Major Longstaff, 32; J. Henderson, Aberdeen, 33, 44; Lubbock Coll, 38; H. White (lent), original by Octavius Hill, 43; Ilfracombe Mus Coll, 50; J. Liddell, 54, 56; The Peabody Museum of Salem, 57; James Randall, 58, 64, 97; W. Domville-Fife, 59, 60; Railway Technical Centre, 68, 80, 123; Attrib Rev Calvert Jones, Swansea, 76, 78, 79, 94; Macfee Coll, 86; Terence Heard, 89; Francis Wayne Coll, 92, 98; F. E. Bowker, 95; Thacker Album, 105; F. Hussey, Ipswich, 107; Hodge Coll, 111, 119; Capt J. R. Robinson, Newhaven, 112; Capt Schofield, 113; Messrs Smiths Suitall Ltd, Ipswich, 120; Foster, Ipswich, 121; Stuart Bruce Coll, 124; Mortimer Coll, 125; Capt A. Petherick, 126; origin unknown, 27, 81, 106.

(b) Photographs of which the National Maritime Museum has prints: Basil Greenhill, 7, 69, 70, 71, 72, 73, 87, 99, 127; H. Oliver Hill, 8, 11, 108; Cardiff Public Libraries, 9; Harold R. Martin, 13, 20, 39, 40; W. D. Wilkinson, 14; Gillis Coll, 15, 30, 41, 49, 53, 77, 91, 96; Bideford Public Library, 19; Miss F. M. Reynolds, 21; W. J. Lewis Parker, 22, 26, 67; George Eley and Michael Staal, 24; Public Archives of Canada, 34, 104; W. J. Slade, 42, 114; B. Shaw, 66; Sutcliffe Gallery, Whitby, 93, 122; Mariner's Museum, Newport News, 100; National Film Board of Canada, 102; Marion Brewington, 103.

The National Maritime Museum can in no case supply prints of photographs in category (b) above. Copies of photographs in category (a) can be supplied only when the museum already possesses an original negative.

SHORT READING LIST

Chapelle, Howard I. *The History of the American Sailing Ships* (New York, 1935)

Cutler, Carl. *Greyhounds of the Sea* (Annapolis, 1961), *Queens of the Western Ocean* (Annapolis, 1961)

Derby, W. L. A. *The Tall Ships Pass* (1937, reprinted Newton Abbot, 1970)

Lubbock, Basil. *The Down Easters* (Glasgow, 1929), *The Last of the Windjammers* (2 vols) (Glasgow, 1927)

March, Edgar J. *Sailing Drifters*, new ed (Newton Abbot, 1969)

Underhill, Harold A. *Deep-water Sail* (Glasgow, 1963)

Villiers, Alan. *The Way of a Ship* (New York, 1953)

INDEX